LOST ROCKERS

Other books by Steven Blush

AMERICAN HARDCORE (Second Edition); 2010
AMERICAN HAIR METAL, 2007
.45 DANGEROUS MINDS (with George Petros), 2005
AMERICAN HARDCORE, 2001

To Alyssa Fisher and Jacqueline Fisher Blush

 powerHouse Books
Brooklyn, NY

Lost Rockers: Broken Dreams and Crashed Careers. Text © 2016 Steven Blush. All images copyright their respective owners and used with permission. All rights reserved. No part of this book may be reproduced in any manner in any media, or transmitted by any means whatsoever, electronic or mechanical (including photocopy, film or video recording, Internet posting, or any other information storage and retrieval system), without the prior written permission of the publisher.

Published in the United States by powerHouse Books, a division of powerHouse Cultural Entertainment, Inc. 37 Main Street, Brooklyn, NY 11201-1021 • telephone 212.604.9074 • e-mail: info@powerHouseBooks.com • website: www.powerHouseBooks.com

First edition, 2016 • Library of Congress Control Number: 2015956495 • ISBN 978-1-57687-766-1

10 9 8 7 6 5 4 3 2 1

Printed by Toppan Leefung Printing Ltd • Printed and bound in China

Front cover photo of Gass Wild by Norman Blake, 1990
Back cover photo of Evie Sands by Emerson Loew, 1972

LOST ROCKERS

BROKEN DREAMS AND CRASHED CAREERS

BY STEVEN BLUSH WITH PAUL RACHMAN AND TONY MANN

EDITED BY GEORGE PETROS · DESIGN BY ERIC SKILLMAN

CONTENTS

AUTHOR'S NOTE

Lost Rockers is an examination of musicians who almost made it, but failed. Some were ahead of their time, some were ill-equipped to deal with success, some simply fucked up. Rock know-it-alls might dismiss my efforts as sonic garbage picking, but that's where many gems are found.

I wrote every word in this book but this project never could have happened without the input of Paul Rachman, Tony Mann, and George Petros. Paul Rachman, with his tireless effort and cinematographic vision, served as the sounding board that helped bring these tales to life. Tony Mann was vital in developing the subject.

None of this could have materialized without the editorial excellence of my good friend George Petros, who deserves more than a thank you for his deft ability to handle my weak sentences and personal issues. And I wouldn't be writing this were it not for the belief and compassion of Alyssa Fisher, who goes to work while I go to write.

Thanks to Craig Cohen, Daniel Power, Will Luckman, Wes Del Val, Miranda Wonder, Craig Mathis, and everyone at powerHouse, especially book designer Eric Skillman. Special thanks to Jim Fitzgerald, the Blush, Radick, Fisher, and Goldstein families, and all the musicians herein. Without you all, there would be no *Lost Rockers*.

STEVEN BLUSH, NEW YORK CITY, 2016

L-R: Gloria Jones, *Share My Love*, 1973. Photo By Chuck Leopold; Chris Robison, *Chris Robison And His Many Hands Band*, 1973. Photo by Hal Wilson; Gass Wild, playing with Public Offenders, CBGB, 2004. Photo by Alan Rand; Evie Sands, *Estate Of Mind*, Haven/Capitol, 1974. Photo by Gene Brownell; All images courtesy of the artist.

ABOUT LOST ROCKERS

BREAKING INTO RADIO'S TOP 40, getting a video on MTV, winning a Grammy Award, and selling millions of songs on iTunes are examples of the upside of the music business. Hit songs, record deals, sexual excess, stretch limos, tour busses, and palatial cribs constitute the trappings of fame. But such successes are incredibly rare.

The quest for rock and roll fame is a Darwinian struggle. The marketplace provides an arena in which many are called but few are chosen. Aspiring wannabe rock stars jockey for position. Some get that record contract. A few of them "make it." Fewer still become famous. The rest wind up in history's dustbin.

"Lost rockers"—those talented and captivating individuals on the verge of stardom who never quite made it—embody the flipside of fame. They played the same venues as their successful peers, performed on the same TV shows, schmoozed the same record labels, appeared in photo shoots and magazine features, and worked with the same agents, managers, and producers. Some lost rockers never had a chance, yet others were so close to fame and fortune they could taste it. The net result was the same: no fame or fortune or artistic triumph—just a lifetime of unrealized hopes and dreams. Their talent, charisma, dedication, intelligence, energy, intensity, and creative credibility amounted to relatively little in the scheme of things.

Radio airplay, press features, and official rock histories are not random constructs—they are controlled functions of the entertainment industry. It's all about money. Powerful behind-the-scenes forces control everything you see and hear regarding pop music. Pushy middlemen enforce a top-down pecking order for the purpose of maximizing profits. Journalists, editors, publicists, and other insiders act as gatekeepers, granting access to the inner sanctum. It's a conservative business disguised as a nonstop party, where everyone takes care of their own. "Losers" don't get their due, while "winners" get more than they deserve.

There are many reasons promising musicians get overlooked. Music is not like sports, where statistics determine success. Stardom is the result of an abstract, ever-changing formula. There's no one-size-fits-all way to make it. Lost rockers possess all the ingredients—perhaps as much as 90 percent of what it takes to succeed. They are, for the most part, commercially viable, well connected, totally driven, and oftentimes a bit heartless. But they're all unlucky, for one reason or another.

On their upward trajectory to fame and fortune, countless musicians get sidetracked by crooked managers, or are rejected by the record-buying public, or are overshadowed by someone better suited for the role, or blow their chance with bad life choices, and then fall into career oblivion. The lost rockers featured in this book became undone by myriad missed opportunities, poor business decisions, lack of focus, dysfunctional personalities, and/or being too far ahead of their time. Some just lacked that "it" factor. And yet many lost rockers, despite their eventual anonymity and frustration, never gave up on music.

At the time of this writing, the lost rockers herein are decades removed from their initial letdowns and can finally be judged on their creative merits, not on contemporaneous circumstances.

All of us, at one time or another, have had dreams of stardom, and we can all relate to these underdogs because we see a bit of ourselves therein. In a way, there's a bit of lost rocker in all of us, whether we dream of being an architect, a poet, or a death-metal vocalist. Lost rockers come in all different colors, creeds, and orientations.

Don't confuse lost rockers with one-hit wonders, obscurities, or D-list rock stars. They were not fleeting shooting stars; they were hardworking individuals whose considerable talents served as grist for the mill, and they received little appreciation or compensation. They willingly partook of the industry "machine" but never profited from it. They harbor deep emotional scars, and little to show for all their efforts.

Today's progressive emphasis on protecting the rights of the wronged doesn't seem to apply to lost rockers. There are no strong unions or activist attorneys to shield them retroactively from creative accounting, no pensions for years spent on grueling tours, no medical insurance, and no retirement plans. And they not only got screwed out of money and fame, but they were also denied the coveted opportunity to say, "I changed the world." Lost rockers can be touchy subjects because they must torturously bare their souls and admit to failure—and the stigma that accompanies it. Herein are personal tales fraught with emotional tragedy. Raw nerves and nails-on-chalkboard revelations abound.

Some lost rockers released songs that did not register until they later got reworked into classics by bigger fish, like Jake Holmes' "Dazed and Confused" (recorded by Led Zeppelin), Gloria Jones' "Tainted Love" (Soft Cell), or Evie Sands' "Angel of the Morning" (Merilee Rush). Other lost rockers inspired the already famous, like Cherry Vanilla's efforts in the service of David Bowie and Andy Warhol. They all worked with iconic musicians, for example Bobby Jameson (Frank Zappa, Rolling Stones), Chris Robison (John Lennon, New York Dolls) or Gass Wild and Johnny Hodge (Sex Pistols, Mötorhead). In every case, something went wrong on the path to stardom.

Personal problems came into play. Jake Holmes didn't possess that killer instinct. Evie Sands got tagged as "difficult." Gloria Jones and Chris Robison made ill-advised choices. Cherry Vanilla and Bobby Jameson got too into subculture to see the broader picture. Gass Wild and Johnny Hodge were too rock for punk, yet too punk for rock.

While researching this book, common threads and shared experiences were uncovered. For example, Gloria Jones, Bobby Jameson, and Jake Holmes each had records on Vee Jay at the same time, but didn't know about one another. Gloria and Evie Sands never crossed paths despite both singing teen-friendly soul music on the LA TV dance shows *Shindig* and *Hollywood A Go-Go*. Evie and Cherry Vanilla as teenagers attended many of the same Allan Freed and Murray The K rock and roll extravaganzas at the Brooklyn Fox and the Brooklyn Paramount, but never ran into each other. Cherry and Chris Robison were both close friends of the late, great entertainer Peter Allen but didn't know each other.

Chris Robison and Jake Holmes hung out in the Greenwich Village folk scene but never met. Bobby Jameson, Chris Robison, and Gass Wild all worked with Keith Richards, but not at the same time. Gass Wilde and Johnny Hodge both inspired the Sex Pistols. Their band the Lightning Raiders played with, and were about to record with, Marc Bolan of T. Rex before he died in a car crash—the car driven by Bolan's girlfriend Gloria Jones. There's also an interesting link to the song "Hey Joe" (popularized by Jimi Hendrix). The song's exact origins remain murky but there are two acknowledged "original" versions: one, by The Leaves, who briefly backed Bobby Jameson, and another by Tim Rose, who Jake Holmes briefly accompanied.

Many conflicting and intangible factors contribute to the magic mix of art and commerce. There's no mathematical success formula when it comes to success in rock and roll.

HARRY BELAFONTE: "Artistic success and financial success are not necessarily mutually exclusive. But I would say this in rebuttal to that thought: more often than not, all the great successes are not artistic."

GLORIA JONES: "It's choice and it's luck. Timing I'm not so sure. I think it's the fortitude and the desire to want more. It has to come back to the love

and to the feelings. The new generation, they're in control of their destiny, they make their own decisions. Back in our day, we didn't have control nor did we trust ourselves to take the risk."

CHRIS ROBISON: "The most successful ones are those that just went for it and didn't really over-think things. They've got this unrelenting drive. It's not about intellect—you just have to do it."

MICHAEL ALAGO: "Not everyone makes it, and that's a tough pill to swallow for most people. I listened to demos for 23 years and I can count on one hand how many hits I might have had. Sometimes there's just no explaining it: they might be charming and have something to say, but it all comes down to the industry machine in which marketing, publicity, radio, and promotion see the A&R person's vision. Sometimes they add up and sometime they don't. It is not a science, and there is no explanation of why some bands work and some don't. You can spend a fortune on all of your artists but it's just the luck of the draw, some things just don't connect with the public the way you planned. The artists and the songs might be incredible, but not everyone makes it."

LEMMY: "You can't win fame. You can't win a contest and be a star. That's not how it works; you have to prove you are a star. Hit makers are only as good as their last hit. We don't play for hits. We play for the music itself, the whole thing."

TERRY REID: "It's all time and place, that's the name of the game. There were a few times in my life that I was definitely in a great place at the right time. But people put a lot of emphasis on stardom and you never know, anything can happen at any time."

CHERRY VANILLA: "If someone were to come along when I was younger and say, 'What would you rather be, rich and nobody or famous and not rich?' I would've said 'Famous! Who needs the money?' Now I have come to realize that being quietly rich is better because you can come and go as you like, and you can have a very lovely time in life. The thing is, if you've never had fame, many people won't realize what they have, even the rich ones think maybe they'd feel better if they were famous."

DOUG YULE: "When Clive Davis was talking about signing my band, he kept referring to 'product.' He was by no means the first one to say that. But it always so offended me that something you pour your heart and soul into, this expression of who you are, gets thought of as product. The business end of it never got the art end of it. If they were on the business side, it was all about business with no feel for the creative. It was not about joy or expression, it was about making money, and they co-opt a lot of people through that. The music business has the ability to do that—they show young artists a good time, which then bends their ethics or morality towards what the music biz wants them to do."

BOBBY JAMESON: "I am just a cog in a wheel, with other cogs, and we are similar cogs. Who are these people and why did these things happen? In my opinion they all deserved to be treated better than this."

BRIAN KEHEW: "It's really a great discovery to find music that should've been heard that probably would've been popular, or at least have a big following or be revered in some way, but instead is completely unknown. It's like digging through the trash and finding a cool lamp or an old book—you never know what you're gonna find. That's what the discovery of lost rockers is all about."

The gulf between the music business and the business of making music is almost impossible to bridge. *Lost Rockers* is a new approach to music history, propelled by digital archiving and nostalgia. It's a re-examination of also-rans long ago relegated to bargain-bin obscurity. Nowadays, thanks to technology, listeners can discover and appraise forgotten music in its proper historical context.

Lost Rockers offers the opportunity for psychological exploration into what it takes to be a "rock star" and what prevented some individuals from attaining that goal. All of these almost-famous folks have gripping stories. They've also made some powerful music that you won't believe you've never heard. A lot of this music was very hard to find, but the search was rewarding.

In America, it's all about second chances, so let's start diggin' through the crates at flea markets, garage sales, and thrift shops to uncover lost gems of our musical heritage. ●

L-R: Bobby Jameson, *Rolling Stone*, 1972. Photo by Richard Creamer; Cherry Vanilla, New York, 1974. Photo by Helmut Newton. From *Lick Me: How I Became Cherry Vanilla*; Jake Holmes, New York, 2011. Collection of Jake Holmes; Johnny Hodge. Photo by Tony Mann; All images courtesy of the artist.

EVIE SANDS

If we're victims of the night
I won't be blinded by the light

— EVIE SANDS, "ANGEL OF THE MORNING"

EVIE SANDS (Evelyn Lourette Sands) was on the verge of fame on more than one occasion, but things never broke right. Evie was born February 26, 1946. The gritty soul singer grew up in a musical, Jewish family in Brooklyn. Her mother was a singer who trained her daughter on piano, guitar, and vocals. Her father ran an Upper East Side eatery through which he made industry contacts. Evie came of age going to Alan Freed and Murray The K's rock and roll shows at Brooklyn's Paramount and Fox Theaters.

"I started singing when I was two years old, and I used to sing myself to sleep. When I was five or six, I used to sneak a radio into my bed and put it near the pillow so no one would hear it, and listen to the music on the different stations. That was the greatest joy in my life. Around that time I recall relatives asking me what I wanted to be when I grew up and I said, 'I want to be a singer.' I didn't know what it meant to be a singer but I knew it was something I wanted to do. It's just been music my whole life.

"I watched whatever I could on television, and listened to the radio constantly. Going to the shows at the Fox and the Paramount, I was suddenly seeing performers do the songs I heard on the radio. I began to understand how this was the right career path for me, something that I could do, too."

She got her professional start in the Brill Building and at nearby 1650 Broadway, a related music publishing building where she cut two demo singles in 1963. "How it started for me was a talent contest. I think a local radio station organized it. Sid Bernstein, the guy who brought The Beatles over, was involved. I entered this contest and got nervous, and got cold feet at first, but ended up doing real well. Sid Bernstein was really kind and very encouraging. So that kind of kicked it off. I found out where all these offices were, and learned to knock on the door and go in and try to either audition or see what it would take to get a foot in the door and get started."

Evie Sands, Blue Cat Records, 1964. Courtesy of Evie Sands.

In 1964, teen Evie teamed with songwriters/producers Al Gargoni ("Brown Eyed Girl") and Chip Taylor ("Wild Thing"), who signed her to Leiber and Stoller's Blue Cat Records.

"I'd seen this young girl on the elevator at 1650 Broadway," Chip Taylor recalls. "Then I heard her voice coming out of Teddy Vann's office and I said, 'Who the heck is that?' They told me it was Evie Sands. I said, 'You mean that little girl I saw?' Then I found out that Al was working with her and I wanted in."

Evie: "I worked with Chip Taylor and Al Gargoni, independent producers who brought my single to the labels of Leiber and Stoller, Blue Cat/Red Bird, who loved it and wanted to put it out. I met Al Gargoni and he brought Chip into it. Technically speaking, here's the story: I did actually meet Chip in an elevator in one of those music buildings with other people. He'd heard those early demos of mine and loved them, which I found out later. In the meantime I wound up getting introduced to Al who worked at a publishing company. Someone introduced us, like, 'Hey, maybe you and this kid can do something together…' So we started working and at a certain point Al called in Chip, because they were friends and collaborators. Al's one of the world's most phenomenal guitarists. You hear about the Wrecking Crew on the West Coast but Al was like the East Coast Wrecking Crew. His guitar is all over songs of the era, the most well know of which is 'Brown Eyed Girl.'

Evie was a pretty, petite, soft-spoken teenager stepping into a ruthless arena of scary businessmen. So she had to learn to push back and let her voice be heard.

"We discovered which were the fly-by-night operations and sleazy places fast, as opposed to the more legit or big-time places. There were records and studios and knobs and instruments; it was all really incredible. The thing is, I kept it to myself, other than a few friends. I never talked about it and I think the reason was because it was so serious to me—and it still is. It was so meaningful to me that I didn't want to talk about it to my friends at school. I didn't use it as a vehicle to become popular. I did it because I had to do music."

"So when Al and I got together with Chip, we recognized each other and he realized I was the singer on those demos he liked. So that's how the three of us started working together. I remember they came to my house and sat with my parents because we had to work on music after school and it wasn't always possible for my mom or my dad or my brother to chaperone. I guess my parents wanted to see if they were trustworthy, and obviously there were. We just cliqued; they were always nice and kind and encouraging and respectful, even though I was just an inexperienced, young kid. I never felt like they ran roughshod over me or coerced me musically. It was a nice repartee we all had. And we're all still close friends to this day."

Her first Taylor/Gargoni-produced single was a song by Trade Martin called "Take Me for a Little While," a Motown-inspired paean to unrequited love and losing one's self-respect ("If you won't love me forever/Take Me for a Little While").

"Trade Martin was a great guitarist and singer-songwriter, and friend," says Al Gargoni. "He had this Supremes-style song, 'Take Me for a Little While.' He knew we were starting to gather material for Evie. He came to our little second-floor office at April-Blackwood Music at 1650 Broadway. Right away it was the feature song we were going to work on. I just remember a cool soulful session and how excited we were by it."

Chip Taylor: "It started out with this great soul singer Evie Sands, young, 15 years old, lovely, and this energy—Al and I had to do something great with her, and finding this Trade Martin song, we were so excited. Back in those days the passion for the business was so great. So that became a wonderful focus for Al and I. That was where it started."

"Trade Martin wrote that song," Evie echoes, "and he played it for us in Chip's office and as soon as I heard it I loved it. It's still one of my favorite records to this day; I really love that one. We knew we could make a great record of it. The recording was great; I can still actually see myself there singing it.

"I was in a car with some friends and it came on the radio. One of my two friends who knew what

Jackie Ross, Chess Records, 1964. Courtesy of Chess Records.

I'd been doing couldn't contain herself and said, 'Oh my God, that's Evie!' and the other people were like, 'Oh yeah, sure.' But that's how it came out. I just said, 'Yeah, it's true...' Then I started touring around the country doing these promotional appearances in different cities. It was always the most amazing feeling to hear myself on the radio because since I was a child I'd been addicted to music on the radio. So to be played alongside The Beatles or Smokey Robinson was so incredible. Three minutes of heaven, basically, just to hear it."

A pre-release of the acetate fell into the hands of a dishonest rep at Chicago's Chess Records. Within 24 hours Chess recorded and rush-released a version of the song with their artist Jackie Ross (hot off a 1964 hit, "Selfish One") and cracked the R&B chart days before Evie's version came out. Radio jocks ignored Evie's rendition as a cover and sided with the popular Ross.

"In a nutshell, what happened was unfortunate," Evie divulges. "They were able to finish the record and get it out and beat our release by a week. I recall opening *Billboard* and *Cashbox*, and after the cover, the first page said, 'Destined to be #1: 'Take Me for a Little While.' I remember thinking, 'Gee whiz, what bad timing. There's a song with the same title as mine.' Later that day I found out it wasn't just the title—it was my recording that had been absconded."

"The way things worked back then," Chip adds, "before a record came out they'd send test pressings to regional markets for the promo men to get excited about what they were about to get. They

sent several of these out and we heard that the reaction was great. In Chicago, the acetate got into the hands of somebody involved in the Chess Records camp. So they stopped the Jackie Ross session and recorded 'Take Me for a Little While,' which was a totally unethical thing to do."

"In the meantime," Evie expounds, "we had legendary music figure George Goldner as a partner with Leiber and Stoller. A whole terrible thing went on behind the scenes. Chess pulled that record off the market by whatever means George Goldner and his people used to convince them. There were a slew of stations playing Jackie Ross, and a lot of them were upset. So the whole thing was ruined; my record could never be some across-the-board national hit. That was my first welcome to the music business."

Chip: "Leonard Chess and George Goldner had a meeting and the Jackie Ross version got sacked. But by then the damage was done. That was the greatest damage done to Evie because not only did they screw her by putting out a test pressing, all the DJs that played Jackie Ross' record now couldn't play it. They were angry, and most of them would never play Evie's record, and that left a bad taste in their mouths about anything else Evie released. It made them look foolish to their audience. So it was a terrible time. One of the heroes of that whole thing was Trade Martin because if Jackie Ross' record went number-one, Trade would've gotten paid and still looked good. But he was on our side from the start. He wanted that record stopped even though that would hurt him. Evie took it all very well. She wasn't devastated. She was just like, 'Let's get the next one.'"

Evie Sands, "I Can't Let Go," Blue Cat, 1965. Later a hit for The Hollies. Courtesy of Evie Sands.

"That wasn't much fun for me," Evie says. "It was pretty depressing. I knew it was a very good record and wherever it got played it did well. It was all very sad—but not enough to make me stop doing music!"

Evie Sands, *The Johnny Cash Show*, June 1969. Uncredited ABC Studios photographer. Courtesy of Evie Sands

I know that it's wrong and I should be so strong
But the thought of you gone makes me want to hold on

— EVIE SANDS, "I CAN'T LET GO"

EVIE'S SECOND BLUE CAT single was 1965's Taylor/ Gargoni-penned "I Can't Let Go." Radio avoided it as a form of revenge for the "Take Me" fiasco. She relentlessly promoted the single, and performed its soulful B-side "You've Got Me Uptight" on *Hollywood A Go-Go*. In 1966, The Hollies had a global hit with their version of the song.

Evie: "Most people don't know my version, but they know other versions. There was still a spillover from radio being upset about what happened behind the scenes with 'Take Me for a Little While,' so again the artist was stuck in the middle. A lot of stations didn't want to play my version as sort of a payback, and it never got a fair

Evie Sands, "Angel of the Morning" ad, Cameo/Parkway, 1967. Later a hit for Merilee Rush. Courtesy of Evie Sands.

shot. Then The Hollies recorded it and they had a hit with it.

"So now here was the second time something happened. It added to this depressing feeling that I had. Interestingly, music was the thing that had always helped me get through feeling sad. Music is still the most important force in my life; nothing can stop me making music. Sometimes life is fair and sometimes it's not, but that has nothing to do with me making music."

Chip: "The way I remember the session, it was missing something. I felt the bottom end wasn't as soulful as 'Take Me for a Little While.' I thought the bass sounded thin. I felt like we missed it. Years later, when I hear it now, I realize I was wrong—it was a helluva record. However we all know The Hollies had the hit with it."

In 1966, Chip got Evie signed to Cameo-Parkway. The powerful label released three singles. The first two—"Picture Me Gone" b/w "It Makes Me Laugh" and "The Love of a Boy" b/w "We Know Better"—had minimal impact. Next came 1967's "Angel of the Morning," her darkly beautiful

vocals ideal for Chip's pop song. Within a week of release, the single was a top AM radio request, and Cameo sold out of the first 10,000 copies. The next week Cameo went bankrupt and the single died. Early the next year, a new recording topped the charts by Merilee Rush & The Turnabouts.

Chip: "I remember the day I wrote it, I remember where I wrote it, and I remember the feeling I had when I wrote it. I'd just watched a war movie on TV about a couple on opposite sides of the fence who might never see each other again, and that was the spirit I took when I sat down at the table. I remember thinking how I didn't like the ballads of the day, that they were soulless, and that I meant to do something meaningful. When I was done, I felt a chill, like I knew it was good. And I knew we were looking for material for Evie. But to tell you the truth, I was nervous Al and Evie might not like the song. At the time I was also working with Billy Vera's sister Kathy McCord. I played it for her but I told her I owed my allegiance to Al and Evie and that she could have it if Evie said no. I always regretted playing it for her. That was wrong."

"We were very excited about it and we were thinking we were gonna have a big, big hit with Evie. It was kind of the same feeling we had before 'Take Me for a Little While.' It came out that Evie was Dusty Springfield's favorite singer, and so many people loved her voice—she had a cult following before 'Angel of the Morning.' The initial reaction to the record was unbelievably great the first week. Then the second week something happens with the record company. Neil Bogart calls me up and says, 'Chip, I hate to tell you this because we just about have a smash hit here but we have to close our doors, we're going bankrupt.' It was a disaster. This one really was hard to take because in the first week it was the number-one requested record in several markets. That's when you knew that you had a hit, when the request lines lit up. It was a real horror."

Evie Sands, Los Angeles, January 1, 1969. Photo by Gilles Petard. Courtesy of Getty Images.

Evie Sands, *Any Way that You Want Me*, A&M, 1970. Collection of the author.

Chip: "I knew Merilee Rush's producers, who asked my permission to cut the song, which they didn't have to. But it was nice that they asked and we said okay. I remember when the record came in. I didn't really give it a chance because in my mind it was Evie's, but I listened to it and then stuck it away in my drawer. The record went up and then down the charts, and like four months later I saw it was still number one on some station in Seattle. So I called them up and said, 'Is this a genuine hit? Isn't Merilee from Seattle?' and they said, 'Yes, but that has nothing to do with it. This is the most requested song we've ever had.' So I convinced the publisher to get behind the record again and revive it. Then it became the hit that went up the charts. I was happy and I loved my song but it was difficult to think about all the things that went on with Evie. I was glad to have it be a hit, but Evie deserved it."

Evie: "That was seriously depressing to me. Those were some hard times. Music was my whole life. I had put all of myself completely into all of this with my true heart and soul. So to have all of these business things, one after the other, always mess it up was like never truly having a chance at bat, so to speak, where I could at least stand up and take a full swing and strike out on my own. Things I did were liked or respected but were restricted due to other forces. I felt like a leaf in the ocean in the business. Even had I had a great manager, they couldn't have prevented what happened to Cameo or that promoter in Chicago. It was a frustrating time, but I just kept going back to the studio to try again."

"The resilience of Evie was amazing," says Gargoni. "She just kept on keepin' on. She was never one to cry about things. In fact, I never, ever saw her throw a tantrum, something you'd expect after the all the rough times she went through. Nothing like that."

After Cameo-Parkway's wipeout came Evie's first hit, "Any Way that You Want Me," a Taylor tune once a hit for The Troggs. *Rolling Stone* hailed it as the top single of 1969 but A&M had no Evie album slated, so the project faded. In 1970, the label finally got an LP together, also called *Any Way that You Want Me*. It featured Sands' hard folk guitar, notably on "It's This I Am, I Find" recorded years later by both Beck and Beth Orton.

Chip: "Al and I were trying to figure out how to break Evie. Finally we chose to cut a song that I'd written that was already a minor hit a few times but not a definitive hit. So Al and I got the passion to rework this for Evie. I wrote a new section for it and I played it for Al and we signed it to A&M. I couldn't imagine a better recording of "Any Way that You Want Me." It was the one I dreamed of. So the single came out, and this was just at the beginning of when the labels started thinking about singer-songwriters and albums without single hits. But it wasn't quite locked in yet. So we have this monster hit-single with Evie,

Evie and friend, Los Angeles, 1969. Photo by Paul Cooper. Courtesy of Evie Sands.

and we had great relationships with the people in New York, but this one was out in Los Angeles with folks we didn't know too well. So our reaction time to make an album to follow up this hit that sells over a half-million copies was very slow. We didn't have an album out for like six to eight months. So even though we had the hit with Evie, we didn't have a follow-up relationship in Los Angeles to really make it happen."

Sands: "I'd just moved to Los Angeles where I had family. A&M was based there and had that great lot over on LaBrea. It was this amazing kind of family atmosphere, a legitimately vibrant community. I was so happy; I really enjoyed my time there. The unfortunate thing that happened was we didn't have an album recorded, and then by the time the album was finally released, it was late the next year. Business all comes down to being able to connect the dots, and all the momentum that came from the 'Any Way that You Want Me' single was already off the charts. So it didn't connect. It was unintentional, but in retrospect it was a terrible mistake to not have done the album first."

Deep in my soul I could feel a quiver When he went down and found that sweet old river

— EVIE SANDS, "LOVE IN THE AFTERNOON"

EVIE REMAINED an in-demand entertainer on TV shows like *The Johnny Cash Show*, *The Glen Campbell Goodtime Hour*, and *The Tonight Show*. In 1969, Cash introduced her singing "How Do You Feel?" with: "Folks, help me welcome a young lady that we think is gonna make it big. She's got the stardust in her eyes, she's got silver bells in her voice, and you'd think she's got electricity in her fingers the way she plays that guitar left handed and upside down. A pretty little girl full of talent, Miss Evie Sands."

Later that year, on the closing skit of an *Everly Brothers Show* episode, Evie teamed with Neil Diamond, The Statler Brothers, and the Everlys on a rendition of "I'll Fly Away." May 1970's *Glen Campbell* set (with actress Leland Palmer and *Gunsmoke* star Milburn Stone) featured Campbell joining Evie, in matching powder-blue polyester suits, in a dueling guitar rave-up of "Swing Low, Sweet Chariot." Before they began, Campbell kissed her on the lips and cooed, "You look nice! And you play guitar too, mmm mmm!"

Evie: "In those earlier days I never found there were problems finding acceptance for females as singers and even as songwriters. It was difficult finding acceptance being a musician or engineer or producer—those were good-old-boy networks. When I began to produce, if I was working with the guys, when we spoke to the suits they'd always look at the guy and not at me. There were exceptions, of course. But even to this day

it's still a kick to me when someone talks of my guitar work because that's the musician in me."

In 1973, Evie teamed with LA-based hit producers Dennis Lambert and Brian Potter. 1974's *Estate of Mind* (Haven/Capitol) recorded at Hollywood's Sound Labs, was the first album on which she wrote or co-wrote all songs, notably the singles "You Brought the Woman out of Me" and the ballad "Love in the Afternoon," later covered in a sensitive manner by Barbra Streisand. To promote the album she did a well-received tour with The Pointer Sisters. Years later, Tom Smucker referenced the album in the *Village Voice* (1/16/78): "One of my favorite records was *Estate of Mind* by Evie Sands. The cover suggested a sort of Carole King, which she wasn't. The songs had no particular message and no stylistic innovations. Just a good pop record."

Evie: "As a songwriter, some things happened. One was that people heard songs on my album and recorded them, so then I was hired to do a few fun things. A song on *Estate of Mind* called 'I Love Making Love to You' got covered a few times. We got a call from Gladys Knight's people saying that she loved this song and wanted to record it, but wanted to adjust the lyrics to get around the overt sexual aspect of it. She asked if we'd write a different lyric, which I was excited to do. Her version was called 'Love Gives You the Power.' My song 'Love in the Afternoon'—Barbra's take was 180 degrees different from my interpretation.

Hers was soft, slow and beautiful, total Barbra. Elvis was working on one of my songs, but he died so it was never recorded."

1979's *Suspended Animation* (RCA) was self-produced by Evie with Michael Stewart of the 60s folk-rock group We Five. The album opened with "Lady of the Night," a duet with Dusty Springfield, and included "Keep My Lovelight Burning" with Toto guitarist Steve Lukather. *Spokane Daily Chronicle* wrote (3/2/79): "One wonders why it has taken singers like Streisand and Dionne Warwick to make hits of Ms. Sands' songs when she just as well could have done it herself. As a matter of fact, if she'd leave the writing to someone else and concentrate on her quality singing voice, maybe more people reading this wouldn't be asking, 'Who's Evie Sands?'"

Evie had it in her mind that she could do everything. RCA executive Charles Koppleman complained to *Billboard* (1/7/78): "Evie is headstrong. She wants to pitch, catch, and run the bases, and it makes things complicated."

Evie Sands, *Estate of Mind*, Haven/Capitol, 1974. Collection of the author.

Evie: "This was still the major label business, and generally speaking, in order to do things, the label typically exerted great control on the artist. Part of the reason I didn't record as much or have as many things out was because I got to a point in my career that I didn't want to be dictated to by business people about my art. Some well-intended folks had suggestions for me. They'd offer money, as long as it was on their terms. That was a big sadness for me because it was always somebody else's idea of what I should be. These people had their careers and jobs and money, and I was one more thing in their day. So it was very easy for them to make suggestions and pass judgment. At the end of the day it would have been me possibly failing and being criticized for art that wasn't mine. I can sing your songs but that's not what's in my heart. So I decided at a certain point I wouldn't do that. But that meant I didn't get as many records made.

"After that album, there were more people interested if I would work under their direction. Either, 'You do these songs,' or, 'Write songs like this,' which was not for me. Why would I want to go out and do something not from my soul? That contributed to my moving on. I got deep into doing studio sessions and producing. But I had a lot of disappointments. I really wanted to record, with every fiber of my being I wanted to record, but all the right deals that came around had those same restrictions. They wanted me to do songs with a certain flavor. But we all know that by the time such a record came out the flavor would be done and there would be a new flavor. Trying to ride the wave of musical fashion can be done, but I'm talking about a far more fundamental thing: putting myself out as an artist. In the 80s I produced a band called Syren. But it was that new wave/post-punk era and what we were doing wasn't that, so labels did not respond positively. Just nothing was coming together the right way."

Evie Sands in the studio, Los Angeles, 1976.
Photos by Richard Germinaro. Courtesy of Evie Sands.

Any way that you want me
Any way that you'll take me

— EVIE SANDS, "ANY WAY THAT YOU WANT ME"

EVIE'S RESURGENCE began after a 1996 encounter with Chip Taylor. The two reteamed with Al Gargoni. They and producer Tommy Spurlock created her 1999 comeback album *Women in Prison* (released by Chip's aptly-titled Train Wreck Records). Through Taylor, Sands befriended U.K. hipsters like Belle & Sebastian, Sonic Boom (of Spaceman 3), and BMX Bandits, all fans who'd been performing her songs.

Chip: "In the 70s, I rarely left New York due to my gambling habit—mostly playing ponies—and had quit music. Evie saw that I started playing shows again and came to see me in LA in 1996. She saw I was inspired and she became inspired again, too. I spoke to Al, and the only people I knew at that point were from the folk scene. We had no contact with pop anymore. I thought that the folk people would like Evie so we did a wonderful album together, *Women in Prison*. It was the same, not skipping a beat. We went down to Nashville and wrote 11 songs in three days and it was a groove."

Evie: "Chip was in town and I went to go see him. We hung out after the show and decided it'd be cool to do an album together again, of course with Al. The album came out in 1999, and the first thing we did was go over and perform in Europe. BMX Bandits had something to do with a gig I was doing in Glasgow with Belle & Sebastian.

"I don't think I was aware of this revival of interest that started in England. It was nice to know that those recordings—that people loved them and had a degree of respect for them. It was an amazing feeling, that whole northern soul movement and all that great fanaticism for music. But what's really fantastic is that it's led to some wonderful friendships in places like Scotland. It's been a joy and I can't wait to go back."

Evie carries on her music from the Hollywood Hills, still playing and producing. She's been married for years, but plays it all close to the vest, providing no deeper information. At the time of this writing, she and LA pop icon Billy Vera have been performing and recording Chip Taylor songs. She was never one to give up, and has no plans to stop making music.

Chip: "In terms of the spirit of music and the tough things that happen in one's past, Evie was never one for giving up, and she's not giving up. Evie has such an unfortunate story—with some difficulties—but she's in the business. And she's still totally breathing this stuff and living this stuff and somehow she's still in there."

Evie: "From that first talent contest on, I have never quit doing music, and I will never quit doing music. Music absolutely is my life. I've always said that it's a blessing and it's a curse. The blessing is the way I hear and feel and experience music, and the joy and privilege of singing for people, to one person or thousands. I absolutely love music as much as I've ever loved music. The thought of being able to sing and play and record and write and perform is so fantastic for me. It's brought me some of the most incredible joy in my life. The curse is because I've never been able to do anything else, there's things in life I would've or could've done in the so-called straight world that would've given me a greater degree of stability. But I cannot ever imagine a time that I won't be making music, as long as I'm in this world." ●

Evie Sands live, Los Angeles, 2006. Photo by John Perry. Courtesy of Evie Sands.

ALAN MERRILL

LR002

I love rock and roll
So put another dime in the jukebox, baby

— THE ARROWS, "I LOVE ROCK 'N' ROLL"

ALAN MERRILL had several dalliances with fame. He was born February 19, 1951 in the Bronx, the son of Aaron Sachs, Benny Goodman's clarinet protégé and Earl "Fatha" Hines' saxophonist. His mother is jazz singer Helen Merrill. He learned the rock game playing in mid-60s Greenwich Village bands like The Kaleidoscope (no relation to Chris Darrow's Kaleidoscope), The Rayne, and Watertown West at Cafe Wha? and other dives.

Merrill's cousin Laura Nyro was like a sister to him. His Bronx high school, William Howard Taft, was across the street from Nyro's parents' apartment. He watched Laura write many of her hits, and in 1968 saw four of those songs simultaneously occupy the top spots on the *Billboard* charts. He auditioned to be in The Left Banke ("Walk Away Renee") and almost got the gig.

That summer, his divorced mother married Don Brydon, vice president of UPI. Brydon was dispatched to Japan during the Vietnam War; that critical posting required heavyweight credentials such as his. Alan and his mother moved to Tokyo. Like a stranger in a strange land, Merrill worked hard to fit in with Japan's parallel-universe pop culture. He struck up friendships with like-minded teens and was able to overcome language barriers enough to

join a Tokyo pop group, The Lead (1968's "Blue Rose" on RCA-Victor Japan).

To the Japanese, Merrill was an exotic foreigner with good looks and musical chops. He was able to go directly to the front of the line of the Japanese pop market. At that time, Western features, physical and psychological, were all the rage in Japan. So here was this fresh-faced American, and before you knew it, he was everywhere.

Merrill made two solo albums for Atlantic Japan: 1970's *Alone in Tokyo* and 1971's English-language *Merrill 1* made him Japan's first Western pop star. *Alone in Tokyo* featured the #1 hit "Namida" ("Teardrops"). He modeled in ad campaigns, starred in a soap opera and in a daytime teen show on which he once hosted Marc Bolan. However, nobody back in America had ever heard of Merrill.

By 1972, he was no longer a teen-idol novelty. He'd become comfortable enough to team up with the drummer Hiroshi Oguchi in the hard-edged glitter-rockers Vodka Collins, noted for 1973's *Tokyo-New York* (EMI Japan) containing the first Japanese rock hit, "Sands of Time." But along with adulation comes resentment, and he had to navigate a political minefield of politeness and backstabbing. The next year, after problems with the band's *yakuza* management, Merrill bolted from Japan. "I had two hits and was supposed to headline Budokan, and I wasn't getting paid enough," he explains. "They thought I had rich parents who would bail me out, but they were wrong."

Merrill moved to London. He teamed with hit producer Mickie Most (The Animals, Jeff Beck) who was putting together The Arrows. Merrill seemed perfect for the gig. In a mere six months, the band scored a Top 10 UK single, 1974's debut "Touch Too Much." The Arrows' fourth single was 1975's "I Love Rock 'N' Roll" that Merrill wrote and sang. He'd written the song in response to the Stones' "Its Only Rock n Roll." The band got a weekly TV show, *Arrows*, on which they performed "I Love Rock 'N' Roll." Despite that success, The Arrows disbanded in 1978 over various issues with Most.

While on a 1976 British tour with The Runaways, Joan Jett saw Merrill do "I Love Rock 'N' Roll" on *Arrows*. She loved the song and worked it into her repertoire. Her 1982 solo version topped the US charts for eight weeks, and remains a rock standard.

Merrill's next London-based band, Runner, dented the American charts for Island Records in 1979 before imploding. Merrill went on to write songs for Lou Rawls, Freddie Scott, and Rick Derringer, with whom he toured and recorded as Derringer's guitarist from 1980–83. But that Derringer lineup had none of the "Rock and Roll, Hoochie Koo" magic.

Work with Derringer resulted in 1985's *Alan Merrill* (Polydor) with Mick Taylor, Steve Winwood, and Dallas Taylor. But the promising effort was overlooked. Merrill spent most of the 80s making a nice living as Meat Loaf's guitarist and is featured on 1987's not-chart-topping *Meat Loaf Live*

Alan Merrill on tour with Rick Derringer, 1982. Photo by Mark Roman. Collection of Alan Merill.

At Wembley (Arista). In 1989 he wrote the theme music for an HBO series, *Encyclopedia Brown*, which was never released. After that, little came his way. Times were lean for Merill, though he could always rely on Joan Jett royalties.

Merrill is now based out of NYC where he still plays rock and roll in relative anonymity. When he goes back to Japan his tours are big. He offers the following about not quite being a rock star: "Being a big rock star is overrated. Most artists I know who've made it as far as to be famous are miserable. My career is one of rock history's more unusual career navigations. My records sell. I'm blessed. I still tour the world. And yes, I still love rock and roll!" ●

CHRIS ROBISON

Lookin' for a boy tonight
I know to some of you out there it may not
seem quite right

— CHRIS ROBISON, "LOOKIN' FOR A BOY TONIGHT"

CHRIS ROBISON grew up around Bridgeport, Connecticut. His musical exploration began on piano, and in fifth grade he picked up the French Horn. Then his life changed after watching The Beatles on *The Ed Sullivan Show*. At age 12, he studied classical guitar under a teacher who pushed him to write his own music and taught him to avoid classical music's stuck-up, snobby aspects. Chris would come to love classical and rock and roll equally.

"The first time I heard 'I Wanna Hold Your Hand,' it raised the hairs on the back of my neck. Rock and roll saved my life. I was already 'alternative' as much as I had these other urges, and was a juvenile delinquent, always in the principal's office."

Chris played in a junior-high-school band with Billy Squier. He saw his first rock show, The Zombies and The Searchers, while working as

a stable hand in Roxbury, Vermont. Then he attended New England Conservatory of Music in Boston, where he spent much time at the notorious club The Boston Tea Party, where he saw incredible concerts with rising stars like Van Morrison, or The Faces with Rod Stewart and Ronnie Wood.

In 1970 Robison played keyboards in a Connecticut band that would become the touring lineup for Steam behind the hit "Na Na Hey Hey Kiss Him Goodbye." Steam was a studio creation of songwriter-producer Paul Leka ("Green Tambourine"). The shady Leka toured a few incarnations of Steam, all previously extant club bands that temporarily changed their name to "Steam" and whose only job, as Robison put it, "was to start with 'Na Na Na Na...' and end the set with 'Na Na Na Na.'" Robison's four-piece ensemble was employed as the second touring incarnation of Leka's Steam. Later, they

Chris Robison with Steam, Mercury Records press shot, 1970. Collection of Chris Robison.

cut their own 45 using the name Steam (1970's "Don't Stop Lovin' Me" b/w "Do Unto Others"), which charted in West Palm Beach and Syracuse. Under Leka's aegis, Robison's Steam lineup toured relentlessly, playing in 28 states in three weeks of one-night stands, media events, and pop festivals.

"Paul Leka was a successful songwriter with a studio on Main Street in Bridgeport. He'd write a hit like 'Green Tambourine' and once he saw it was getting airplay, he'd go out to the local clubs and find a band doing covers and say, 'Youse guys are The Lemon Pipers.' So they'd go on the road and play. Same thing with Steam. 'Na Na Na Na...' was the flipside to the single but it became a monster hit. So he got a Connecticut band and said, 'Youse guys are Steam and you're going on the road.' The band on the album cover, those guys burned out after like ten months, so I was in the second Steam. Otherwise we played original music we recorded ourselves.

"The little lady who booked us would get $4,000 a night and scoop $1,000 off the top. She owns an island someplace now. Then Paul Leka and his partner and another person would each take 15 percent, and then we'd get the rest and have to pay our own way. One-night stands in towns like Enterprise, Alabama and Washington, North Carolina. We almost died when a wheel came off on the interstate. In Lincoln, Nebraska, they had a poster of the first band lineup and the owner noticed. He yelled, 'I paid for something and didn't get what I paid for!' He was ready to kill us. In order to keep his feathers from being ruffled, we went back and played that club again for free. That was my first taste of really hard work on the road."

Robison played in Elephant's Memory, on 1969's gold-certified *Midnight Cowboy* soundtrack ("Old Man Willow," "Jungle Gym at the Zoo") and 1969's *Elephant's Memory* (for Buddah) with the Latin-flavored minor hit-single "Mongoose."

"I quit Steam and joined Elephant's Memory because they needed a keyboardist. I went to Magnagraphic Studios on Bedford Street, the same place where years later Elephant's Memory met John Lennon. I learned a lot from those guys. Stan Braunstein was a terrific sax player. He'd played with all the salsa big bands, like Tito Puente, who he had some incredible stories about.

"Elephant's started out being produced by Wes Farrell, who did *The Partridge Family*. At first they were this bubblegum act. But when they had enough money they tried to have their own band commune house and recording studio in Spring Valley, New York. They came home one night from a gig and it was burned to the ground. Over the next few days they heard folks saying, 'We took care of those hippies...' That's when they became radicalized. They played a Black Panthers

Chris Robison, Steam, 1970. Collection of Chris Robison.

rally in Hartford infiltrated by the FBI. There was tear gas thrown and a riot. Everyone got off the stage, but Allen Ginsberg stayed and recited his whole long poem. When I was in the band we played for the FMLN, the Puerto Rican Liberation Front, and stuff like that. So yeah, it was pretty political."

In 1971, Robison moved to LA to write, record, and play (mostly uncredited) with "The Next Hendrix," Velvert Turner. 1972's *Velvert Turner Group*, made with noted producer Tom Wilson, came out on Woodstock-star Michael Monarch's Just Sunshine Records.

"The first time I met Velvert Turner was at The Stable Inn in the Village. He swooped down in this huge rented limo and came in. He looked just like Jimi Hendrix except he was like a foot taller. In fact he was actually Jimi's little friend

before and after Jimi made it, and he had stories that'll never get aired. If you look at old Hendrix movies, you'll often see a really tall skinny guy like a head taller than Jimi dressed the same way. That was his little brother, sidekick, protégé—that's all I'll say about it. He was on an East Village rooftop when Jimi said, 'Velvert, I have to leave, I have to go to England, because I'm gonna make it big. But I'll be back for you.'

"So Velvert took me to that hotel, across from Madison Square Garden, and we spoke all night long. He was trying to talk me out of Elephant's Memory. I'd only been in that band for about nine months and they just had their hit 'Mongoose' and I really liked them. But Velvert talked about going to Hollywood, the Coast, bye bye Miss American Pie and all that, so I took him up on it. The next day I went to the Elephant's Memory rehearsal and told them, and it did not go over well. So after an Elephant's gig in Columbus, Ohio, I had an airplane ticket sent to me by the producer Tom Wilson. Tom had previously screwed up because Chas Chandler of The Animals tried to get him to work with Jimi Hendrix in 1966 but Wilson said, 'I'm in the music business, not in the carnival business. I'm not gonna see some guitarist play with his teeth!' So at the end of his tour, Chas took Jimi to England, and the rest is history.

"So I got a flight to LAX, and Tom Wilson met me with his Porsche. He looked at my clothes and said, 'Man, we've got to get you some new threads.' The bassist Scotty Niles went on to be

in The Knack, and Tim McGovern the drummer became the guitarist in The Motels who did that song 'Only the Lonely,' so when we made the record, there were great musicians. We rented a house in LA from Flo and Eddie of The Turtles."

The Velvert album flopped. After that year-long fiasco, Robison moved back to the Village. He went to visit his buddy, Elephant's drummer Rick Frank. The other guys were there, and asked him to rejoin the band. Robison told them he was spent after the Velvert mess and needed time off. Chris was in and out of Elephant's Memory a few times because he was pursuing other opportunities. During one of these absences, John and Yoko happened to hire the band. Had he been a member of the band that day, he would've been part of Lennon lore.

"I swear it was only a few days later, I went back to Rick Frank's house on West 10th Street. I got up there and he pulled me in the door. And with these wild, crazy eyes he said, 'Chris, we're John

L: Chris Robison, New York, 1974. Photo by Hal Wilson. Collection of Chris Robison.

R: Elephant's Memory, Apple Records, 1972. Chris wrote songs on this album produced by John and Yoko. Collection of the author.

Chris Robison, promotional flyer for *Chris Robison And His Many Hands Band*, Gypsy Frog Records, 1973. Collection of Chris Robison.

Lennon's band.' I was in stunned silence and said, 'Well, I'll come back in the band now.' He went, 'No, no, no, we can't do that. John's calling the shot's now; we're John's band.'

"Because of their politics, when John and Yoko came to New York, Abbie Hoffman and Jerry Rubin said, 'Have we got a band for you!' John and Yoko brought the band to the studio on Bedford Street. John Lennon took out his guitar, and broke into 'Blue Suede Shoes.' Elephant's were amazing at old-school rock and roll, so he said, 'You're my band.'"

Elephant's Memory backed John on his *Some Time in New York City* album and Yoko on her *Approximately Infinite Universe*, and the couple's Madison Square Garden shows. In return, John

and Yoko produced June 1972's *Elephant's Memory* for Apple Records (not to be confused with 1969's *Elephant's Memory* on Buddah). The LP included tunes cowritten by Robison.

"I never got to hang out with John at the Chinese restaurant or go onstage or jam in rehearsal with him," Chris explains. "But Elephant's invited me to the Record Plant East on West 44th Street where John and Yoko were producing *Elephant's Memory*. Some of those songs were cowritten with me so I got to meet John and Yoko, I got to put on the headphones with John and sing background on 'Baddest of the Mean.' I looked at that album recently and it listed 'Power Boogie,' written by me, Stan, and Rick and it said 'John Lennon, extra guitar.' So John Lennon played guitar and sang backup on my song. That's pretty good."

Lookin' for a chicken can't find none
Where do I go to find me some?

— CHRIS ROBISON, "DOWN IN NEW YORK"

CHRIS, AN AVOWED "PANSEXUAL," made one of the first openly gay rock albums back when, as he says, "gay and rock didn't go together." Chris produced and played all of the instruments on his 1973 solo debut *Chris Robison and His Many Hands Band*, put out by his manager Hal Wilson's Gypsy Frog Records. The double-entendre title referred to Chris' musical dexterity. The album was recorded for $2,000 in a defunct studio near The Bottom Line.

"Oh yeah, the solo records. This was right after The Stonewall Riots. You can't imagine today what it was like to deal with gayness or bisexuality. David Bowie and Lou Reed played 'peekaboo' with their lyrics and dressed up. I even remember a Johnny Winter album where he got all decked-out. But I just came right out and did songs about gay experiences. All these kids thought of rock in terms of straight sexuality; there wasn't anything else out there. So I felt it was my duty to do an album with such songs. And I didn't really give a fuck what happened.

"Hal Wilson picked up on what I was doing right away and said, 'Just do some of these songs and we'll record it ourselves and put an ad in *After Dark* magazine.' This was after all the majors turned us down. Hal was well known in the industry, and got me an audition at RCA here in New York. I passed the audition and the second stage was in the studio, where I cut the song 'Jimmy Monroe' with these two great engineers who worked with Lou Reed. Then I had one more audition. But in the final analysis they said, 'He's a good artist, we like him a lot. But we already have David

Bowie and Lou Reed,' who was quite gay at that time, at least he sort of faked it. So Hal said, 'Oh, I get it RCA, you don't want a third fag on your roster.' We ran into that trouble a lot."

Robison's debut solo album featured the Fire Island anthem "Lookin' for a Boy Tonight"—which he performed at the first gay pride concert at Washington Square Park in June 1973, an event headlined by Bette Midler.

"I was riding on the back of a bus from Times Square down to the Village," Chris recalls. "These lyrics came to me, and I didn't have to rewrite any of 'em, and I thought it'd be good to do a shit-kickin' version of this song: 'Lookin' for a Boy Tonight/I know to some of you out there it may not seem quite right/But I am not the only one who knows your own sex can be fun/That's why I'm Lookin' for a Boy Tonight/Girls can be alright in their way/As long as you don't have them every single day/Variety is the spice of life and you all know that's true/That's why I'm Lookin' for a Boy Tonight.'

"I played at Washington Square Park on a four-foot tall stage in front of the arch. It was 1973 and it was a big gay celebration with all these famous people. Vito Russo [gay activist] said I could only do one song, so I went up there with my band and did 'Looking For A Boy Tonight.' It was a hot day and the place was jam-packed. And everyone started booing me, yelling 'Straight! Straight!' Because at that time, it was the infancy of gay lib and people hadn't really figured things out. Now it's LGBT,

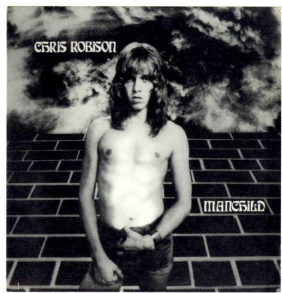

Above: Chris Robison, front and back covers of *Manchild*, Gypsy Frog Records, 1974. Photos by Hal Wilson. Collection of the author.

Opposite: Chris Robison, *Manchild* contact sheet. Photos by Hal Wilson. Collection of Chris Robison.

but back then all those people were at each other's throats, always calling each other names. So when I went up there, playing loud rock music and not doing camp and not dressed in high heels or whatever, I got a really negative reaction."

Next came 1974's *Manchild* with songs like "You'll Never Get Cheated on by Your Hand." The album had a cover shot of Chris in his long blond locks with no shirt on, and there are other photos of him with his young friend Tony Pony covered by just a guitar. The songs explored similar themes, this time backed in the studio by members of Elephant's Memory. Suffice it to say this album did not tear up the charts, but it did have a minor critical impact.

"We had to do it all ourselves, but once we put out the album I became the poster child for gay music. I was on the cover of *Michael's Thing* and *Gay*

Times in London for two weeks. I happened to be on tour with Elephant's Memory, and when I'd leave them to hang out in London, on every other streetcorner I'd be staring at magazine cover shots of me! It was really very odd."

In those days, Chris got good press. *Cashbox* (3/73) crowed: "Homosexual rock really comes out of the closet here in musical genres from folk to hard rock." *After Dark* (2/73) declared, "Robison is honest about his sexuality, neither trying to shock nor exploit homosexuality." *Gay Sunshine* (#20) read: "A sensitive, good-looking guy and a fine musician whose songs are as openly gay as he is—a rare phenomenon in the rampantly commercial, equivocal field of popular music—Robison is a poet among poseurs." But he was too ahead of his time. No major label or mainstream media would touch Robison.

"I think the record companies have encouraged people to play that down all along. I mean, you'd be surprised... Little Richard, people think of him as just a crazy old entertainer, but he's a big old queen. When he played at The Whiskey A Go-Go in Hollywood, after the show my girlfriend went up to a party at the hotel and found him in bed with his guitar player. But it's strange because I can act as straight as anyone, but at some point I do become real with somebody. I don't say, 'Hi I'm Chris Robison and I'm bisexual.' I usually wait for the first foul anti-gay joke to come up and then say, 'Hey, I don't like that. Not only are some of my best friends gay, but I am too!'

"But it did affect who'd talk to me and who would not. When I was the poster child I was doing a radio interview and this guy called up to say, 'I've got a Brooklyn newspaper called the Jewish something or other. I'm a rabbi and I'd like to do a feature on you.' We met at The Bottom Line on Mercer Street, and sat at a table and he began to interview me with his pad and paper. The next thing you know his hand is under the table trying to grab me. My friend, the drummer of Steam, who was there and quite stoned at the time, was laughing hysterically. I was the only one dumb enough or brave enough to come out, so I was a target for people looking to explore that side of themselves. Stuff like that was probably the worst—but nothing too bad."

Through producer Ron Johnsen Chris got hired to play on a demo for the group Wicked Lester at the Jimi Hendrix-founded Electric Lady Studios, before they became KISS.

"I joined this jazz-rock group RPM that caught the ear of one Ron Johnsen who was producing Wicked Lester. Ron needed a keyboard player, so I got the job. I remember

KYOTO JAPAN 8/15 Bob

ニューヨーク・ドールズ

静岡・稲葉るみ子

Top: Chris Robison, New York Dolls, Kyoto, Japan, August 1975. Polaroid by Bob Gruen.

Bottom: Illustration of Robison with New York Dolls, *Music Life* Magazine, Japan, 1975. Collection of Tony Mann.

a call from Gene Simmons saying, 'Here's my number, and if someone answers the phone and they don't speak English, that's my mother, so just yell, 'Gene! Gene!'

"Just like any other gig, I played my parts and dummied up a bit because Gene didn't want anything too serious. I just recall a lot of A-minor chords in the songs. During one of the breaks by the coffee machine, Gene told me his concept for the band. He said they were gonna dress up and wear makeup with dance steps and explosions. I just said, 'Okay Gene, that sounds great.' I was cornered and couldn't get out of the room fast enough.

"Five months later, I got invited to some special reopening of The Fillmore East that KISS head-lined. Half the people were laughing and jeering, and the other half were loving it. I thought it was pretty good. So after the show was over I waited around in the lobby. There I ran into Gene and Paul [Stanley]. They said, 'Chris, what did you think of the band?' And I didn't register that it was them. So I said, 'I thought it was a bit cartoonish.' And I'll never forget the look I got—this, 'I'll show you' kind of thing. We had a good laugh about it years later when I was in the Dolls and we played together in New Orleans. He knew what to do and he did it. He wanted to keep the keyboards simple because he felt that he'd lose the audience."

Through Elephant's Memory drummer Rick Frank's managers Steve Leber and David Krebs, Chris got a gig playing keyboards in a late lineup of the New York Dolls. That 1975 incarnation of the band—derided by insiders as "the Doll-ettes" and omitted in most "definitive" Dolls histories—was based around original members David Johansen and Sylvain Sylvain. The Robison lineup played across the South, mostly in the middle of a triple-bill with Lynyrd Skynyrd and a budding KISS. They did a five-date tour of Japan, at the apex playing to 55,000 screaming girls at Tokyo Baseball Stadium with Jeff Beck and Felix Pappalardi. In all, Robison was in the Dolls less than a year.

"I went to this audition. It was the New York Dolls. They had just gotten an offer to do Japan. People kept dying in that band—you know, overdoses—so they thought they'd try out something different with a keyboard player. I didn't really know the songs but I can pick things up fast. The asked me to come back the next day, and after the second audition they didn't say anything. In the *Let It Be* movie, John says, 'I hope we passed the audition.' So I said to David, 'David, did I pass the audition?' He turned around and gave me that great shit-eating grin of his and said, 'Yeah!' And that was it.

Chris Robison and David Johansen with Andy Warhol, Max's Kansas City, 1975. Photo by Bob Gruen.

"When I was in the Dolls, they had to assemble a new lineup because of this gig offer in Japan. But the new members, like myself, had all this new material with these new ideas; it sounded and looked different, and there was a bit more musicianship going on. We were moving away from camp. I remember after the first show in Japan, David pulled me aside and grabbed my hand and said, 'Thanks, man.' That's why what ended up happening was all so sad in my eyes.

"One of my life's great regrets is that still to this day I don't know exactly how I got bounced out of that band. I remember getting really drunk, and Syl came over to my house and I said some words, whiskey words, not based on anything. I must have put them down or something. The next day there was a gig at Cobo Hall in Michigan to start a big tour. I woke up at two in the afternoon and they'd already gone. Apparently I said stuff like I wasn't gonna do it, but that wasn't based on reality. I'm sorry guys, it was just a drunken moment.

"After I got bounced from the New York Dolls, I felt so bad," Robison concedes. "I felt like I let down the team. You want to be there, be there on time, and do the gig. But they went to Cobo Hall and David told me later, 'That was so fucked up because we could only do a few songs on a moment's notice with this new guy, and you fucked us up bad.'

"So Mark Ianello from the neighborhood market said, 'Yo Chris, what are you gonna do now?' I said, 'God protects drunkards and fools. I'm starting my own band. I'm gonna call it Stumblebunny and I'm gonna book it now.' I went to Max's because I knew the booker, and told him I had a new band. So three months later, we had this show and still no band. Then I heard of Sammy Brown the drummer, and knew he was black and that'd give us some class. Three days before the gig my friend offered me his guitarist for the night—that was David White. With Pete 'Street' Jordan and myself coming from the New York Dolls, there was a bit of momentum. We ironically ended up rehearsing in the same place as the Dolls, which was kind of interesting. That was a fun band."

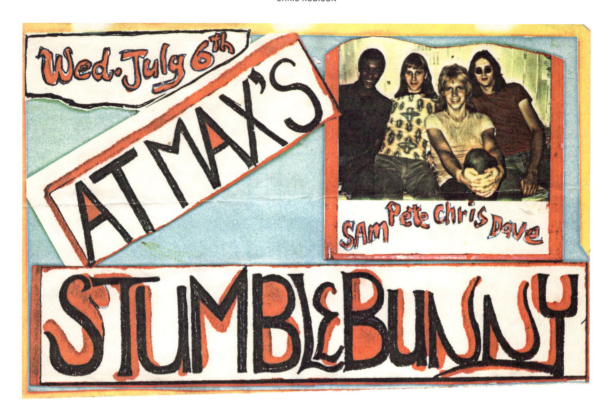

Chris Robison, Stumblebunny flyer, Max's Kansas City, July 6, 1977. Collection of Chris Robison.

Hit producer Richard Gottehrer re-worked the EP's "Tonite" as a 1978 hit in Germany, backed by Robison and his Elephant's friends Stan Bronstein, Rick Frank, and Jerry Van Gank. That song had originally been released in 1974 on Buddah as the Chris Robison single "I'm Gonna Stay with My Baby Tonight," which came out just as the label folded. Then the producers took the tune to Europe, where they had a #1 hit by replacing Chris' vocal tracks with those of Tony Sherman, a Chicago soul singer popular in Holland. The song has since been recorded at least 33 times, most notably a 1976 disco version by George McCrae ("Rock Me Baby"). Robison wrote what he considers his greatest song, atypically, after a sexy night with a woman.

"I wrote this song 'I'm Gonna Stay With My Baby Tonight' after an evening with an incredible girl named Jewel; not *the* Jewel, but another one. I played it over the phone to Hal Wilson who was up on 72nd Street and he said, 'We have to record that right away.' It just came to me all at once. Girl or boy, it wasn't so much the gender as the person.

"Hal Wilson, who suggested I do the gay record, which was successful in its own way, was still trying to peddle that. I told him about 'Tonight' which I wrote in seven minutes. I got the guys from Elephant's Memory to record it with me, and it came out great. The music publisher Bob Reno took it to Europe and they added Tony Sherman's vocals. I still get royalty checks for it from Holland. It was done many different ways afterwards. It was done in South Africa by this band Sticky Patch. George McCrae did it. It was recorded by Ronnie Spector. Produced by Genya Ravan with Cheetah Chrome of the Dead Boys on it. The song's been published in every country except for the United States and Canada. But it's a classic song and will be a hit again."

A version of the song led off Stumblebunny's 1979's *While You Were Out* (cut at Plaza Sound with Gottehrer) released only on Phonogram Germany. Then 'Bunny embarked on a less-than-successful German tour with The Hollies.

During that era, Robison also worked with Keith Richards, Link Wray, and Robert Gordon (Farfisa on 1980's *Bad Boy*).

"I made a good sum of money playing studio gigs with Keith Richards and Papa John Phillips. Keith Richards told a judge he was in Switzerland getting blood transfers when in fact he was detoxing here. I took that money and did recording of my own. That's how we printed and mastered and stamped the *Stumblebunny* four-song EP. We went up and down Tin Pan Alley and gave them out like Frisbees to every label. About a week later Richard Gotthehrer called up and said, 'I like the song and I'm impressed how you put this all together.' He signed us without ever really hearing us." Needless to say, Stumblebunny, despite hard work and a solid material, never became a household name.

After many years of near misses in the music business, Chris had become hardened and cynical. He burned bridges with his booze-induced rages and poor decisions, like the ugly drunken incident that got him fired from the Dolls. Or suing David Johansen for not crediting Chris' songs from those Dolls jams that ended up on David's 1978 solo album. Chris won the suit

and money and credit, but lost in the court of public opinion. He became a pariah of sorts, and then David retaliated by never again playing those tunes.

"That was a pyrrhic victory, one of those things when you win but you lose. It was due to Velvert Turner, who ripped me off wholesale; he stole everything. That's why I was so strict about never getting ripped off again. So when we wrote these Dolls songs, I took time to make a mental note when I put something in there, and then I went and copyrighted it for safekeeping. I don't think David did it maliciously. When it came time for their solo careers, he took half the songs and Syl took the other half to his band, The Criminals. But I got a lawyer and I sued David. That made me unpopular. That was not a good move, but it got me enough money to go to London for a while. I've spent more effort on songs I cowrote with ideas I came up with off-the-cuff than I do pushing my own records. Why should I care if my name wasn't on 'Funky But Chic'? You're supposed to always give credit, and I always gave credit."

"I had a lot going on but I jumped around a lot. I had some great luck being able to jam with Dylan and to work with Gene Simmons at Electric Lady Studios. I didn't do so well with the Dolls. But maybe it was just excesses, getting caught up in substances and alcohol. I had a terrible alcohol problem. I went to rehab like 30 years ago. I always said I wanted to raise kids and have a family but I knew I needed to stop doing all that first. So it just got kind of got old for me after that.

"Look, if you work in a coal factory, you could come down with black lung. If you work in rock and roll, you may well just come down with an addiction, and that's what happened to me. For me not to pick up drinking would mean to stay away from people, places and things, including rock and roll."

And the future looks mighty fine for us
If it's anything like tonight
There won't ever be a moment like tonight

— CHRIS ROBISON, "I'M GONNA STAY WITH MY BABY TONIGHT"

IN 1981, ROBISON MARRIED a woman. After a quickie wedding near Washington Square Park, they relocated to his native state of Connecticut, where he raised two boys.

"The little lady got pregnant, and we got married in a taxi on West 9th Street. It was the same corner I first met her on when we were both hailing a cab and realized that we lived in the same building at Waverly and 6th. So we thought it'd be funny to get married hailing a cab. The driver was Peter Allen, the entertainer, who I knew. David White filmed it from the front seat of a Checker cab at some astrological moment when the planets aligned. Then we had our reception at a Chinese restaurant around the corner.

"I was Mr. Mom while my wife went off to work, and quite content to live in the suburbs of Stamford with my two boys. I took my cues from John Lennon, who dropped out for a while to raise Sean. The best thing to happen for me in my life was becoming a father; it gave me a chance to relive my childhood. And like John, I insisted on changing every diaper and staying home with the kids. Success is when your son gets chosen by the PTA to recite his essay. To see my kid on the Internet doing music, that is success."

Robison paid the price for being a gay rock pioneer: "Oh yeah. I did. My idea for the record was just to let everyone know its okay to be this way. Most people had the good sense not to talk about it, whereas I had this fucking album follow me around for over 30 years between two marriages, two kids and stepkids, and my music students' parents worried if they'd see this. I'm still conflicted by it all. I think I'm my own worst enemy. I never tiptoed around. I had to search to find myself in a hetero world.

"I mean, you can't go back and spell out the reasons why record companies didn't want you. But being a rock and roller, and sleeping all day and playing all night wasn't too bad then. It's only a problem now, 30 years later, like when my first ex-wife brought my first album to court in a custody fight. The kids lived with me the whole time when I was Mr. Mom, but she came to threaten me with the judge. Luckily my kids were raised very liberal. When my Dexter was in his senior year he said, 'Dad, I went on the Internet and there's this song called 'Looking for a Boy Tonight' by Chris Robison.' I said 'Yup Dex, that's me.' There was a moment of silence and then he said, 'Cool!' That's how the kids got introduced to that side of me."

In the 90s, Robison and musical partner Steve Farrell played children's music as Papa Chris & Steve. At the time of this writing, Chris gives piano lessons in Connecticut and plays around NYC in a reformed Stumblebunny. The self-professed closet architect maintains a few of his old rock and roll trappings, like shaggy hair and a

Chris Robison, early-80s family polaroid with his infant son Dexter Scott. Collection of Chris Robison.

muscle car. His son Dexter carries on the family tradition, recording music under the name Dexter Scott.

"It was difficult when I left the city and all of my rock and roll friends. I turned on the fledgling MTV and there were three videos in a row by bands I used to be in. That was tough. I may not have always been active in music but I never stopped writing songs.

"I went to a shrink once—talk about obsessions—and he said, 'Chris, if you don't do music, you're gonna die, either physically, or spiritually, or emotionally.' So I kept writing songs and never really stopped." ●

GINGER BIANCO

LR004

Cocaine Elaine, she never complains
She's so aware, you know she likes to share

— ISIS, "COCAINE ELAINE"

GINGER BIANCO was likely the first female rock drummer. She was the quintessential New York broad: an alpha female, a feisty, petite brunette able to hold her own in the rapacious music business. She was a rock and roll pioneer who worked incredibly hard and did everything right, but at the end of the day she didn't receive her due.

Bianco co-founded Goldie & The Gingerbreads, recognized as the first all-girl rock group. Stylish in beehive hairdos, gold lame, and stilettos, the ladies—drummer Ginger "Gingerbread" Bianco (Panebianco), singer Genyusha "Goldie" Zelkowitz, guitarist Carol MacDonald (Shaw), and Hammond B-3-er Margo Lewis (Crocitto)— signed to Atlantic in 1964 after Ahmet Ertegun saw them perform at fashion photographer Jerry Schatzberg's party for Warhol superstar Baby Jane Holzer. The future looked bright.

The band's first big gigs were at the Peppermint Lounge and the nearby Wagon Wheel. That's where Animals singer Eric Burdon and future Jimi Hendrix manager Michael Jeffreys saw them perform at an Atlantic party for The Rolling Stones. Burdon said, "I was stunned to find such a black sound could be produced by a group of white girls." That encounter resulted in various British tours with The Animals, Stones, Kinks, Who, and Hollies. 1965's minor hit "Can't You Hear My Heart

Beat" (Decca UK), produced by Animals keyboardist Alan Price, fared better when redone in 1966 by Herman's Hermits. The 'Breads crumbled in 1968 due to mismanagement and changing times. The male-dominated pop cognoscenti often dismissed them as a novelty act.

Bianco then formed Isis, named for the Egyptian patroness of nature and magic. The brass-driven, funky, female eight-piece was like a lesbian Blood, Sweat & Tears. The ladies, a blend of classically trained musicians and self-taught neophytes, signed to Buddah in 1973 after a *Rolling Stone* feature and a gig at Trude Heller's in the Village. 1974's *Isis*, featuring a cover picture of the ladies wearing only metallic body paint, cracked the *Billboard* charts at #87. Of that Shadow Morton-produced, David Bowie-endorsed LP with songs about women loving women, *Mademoiselle* raved, "It will slam you over."

Critics were not as receptive to 1975's jazzier *Ain't No Backin' Up*, recorded in New Orleans with Allen Toussaint. *Milwaukee Journal*'s Pierre-Rene Noth wrote (7/2/75): "Toussaint has taken Isis and mellowed, funked and souled them into a nonentity. Let's hope this venture teaches Isis the first lesson of women's lib: To thine own self be true." Bianco quit before '77's slicker *Breaking Through*, produced by 60s pop star Len Barry.

Ginger Bianco in Isis, a Sapphic funk group from Greenwich Village. Buddah Records album covers of 1974's *Isis* and 1975's *Ain't No Backin' Up Now*. Courtesy of Ginger Bianco.

Goldie & The Gingerbreads, the first all-girl rock band, Ginger with drum sticks. New York, 1963. Photo by James J. Kriegsmann. Courtesy of Ginger Bianco.

Despite great gigs opening for the likes of Aerosmith, Beach Boys, Lynyrd Skynyrd, ZZ Top, and Dr. Buzzard's Original Savannah Band, Bianco and Isis never seemed to strike a chord with finicky audiences. Fame never came. Among Isis' missteps was insisting on headlining over a nascent KISS at The Coventry in Queens and getting blown off the stage.

Bianco spent the 80s and 90s enduring a string of personal and professional setbacks. She tried to break back into music, but the deck was stacked against her. She was a demanding perfectionist and she scared a few people away.

The rise of punk and new wave girl groups did not rekindle interest in her work. A few promising musical projects fizzled. In the oos she tried to make a documentary film about her life, but she fell out with her production partner, who never returned her archives. Bianco has undergone

her fair share of lean periods. At the time of this writing, she works at a Home Depot in suburban Westchester County.

Ginger Bianco, in the Gingerbreads and Isis, was a woman ahead of her time. She and her bands tried to break the prevailing mold, and make the audience see beyond gender. So when their records sold little and success didn't come, it wasn't just she and her bandmates failing to chart, it was like the public rendering its verdict on women in rock. Bianco stuck to her vision and did things her own way and never wavered. But back then there was no place in the music business for strong women unafraid to express their Sapphic side. One can only imagine that if the drummer were straight, perhaps she would've been a rock star.

Ginger snapped: "Isis was an intimidating band. We were phenomenal. We played at the Orange Bowl; we played everywhere. Then, from the first album to the second, there were lots of bad things and painful issues, turns of events, and drugs in motion. I hated the second album. It had a photo of me in a spice jar, and the sound was totally wrong. Allen Toussaint tried to change our sound, and that was the beginning of the end. Isis broke down barriers, but it was very aggressive, and we really turned some people off." ●

BRETT SMILEY

LR005

I've gone so crazy, I'm a certified nervous wreck
A little bit eccentric, screaming at the discotheque

— BRETT SMILEY, "VA VA VA VOOM"

BRETT SMILEY was almost a glam-rock star. One critic even called him "The Most Beautiful Boy in the World." He was raised in Washington, Indiana until age 12, when his mother got divorced and moved the children to New York, where the young Smiley achieved early fame on Broadway as the youngest-ever star of *Oliver* and then with spots on *The Ed Sullivan Show* and in TV commercials. The family followed his career to Los Angeles, where he attended junior high with, and befriended, Michael Jackson. By age 16, he joined the pop-rock band Sky, whose guitarist Doug Feiger later rocked in The Knack.

Smiley's first manager, radio DJ Russ Gibb (notorious for 1969's "Paul is Dead" hoax) set up a cocaine-fueled deal with early Rolling Stones' producer Andrew Loog Oldham, who'd worked with Sky when they toured England. Andrew secured Brett a six-figure solo deal with the London-based Anchor label. Oldham had grand plans to make Smiley the next Bowie. Anchor weighed in with a 1974 single, Smiley's T. Rex-inspired "Va Va Va Voom" (the label also released the band Ace's smash "How Long" with a pre-Squeeze Paul Carrack).

Despite numerous British TV appearances, glossy ads, and flashy billboards, Smiley's glittery single turned to pixie dust. One low point was a September 19, 1974 performance on *The Russell Harty Show* before which, in the dressing room, Oldham warned a smashed Smiley to never mix Valium, sleeping pills, and booze. The performance was a disaster. Afterwards Harty expressed concern for the singer's well-being.

Smiley returned to America to record *Breathlessly Brett*, envisioned by Oldham to be an unparalleled pageant of Broadway, Hollywood, and glam rock. They completed the album, but it got shelved when the fly-by-night label folded. The singer was devastated. His downward spiral had begun.

Brett Smiley was a young, impressionable, good-looking kid on a great trajectory for fame who got waylaid by drug dealers and scam artists. Andrew Oldham was a parasitic character, despite his Svengali-like reputation. None of his post-Stones projects worked. Oldham took a promising young American pop singer and mismanaged him, putting him in a drug-and-booze netherworld that almost destroyed the aspiring star.

Smiley spent the late 70s and early 80s focusing on hard drugs, B-movie roles, and rejected demos in Nashville and Los Angeles. Somehow he made it back to New York where he became a regular at CBGB, playing with his junkie-punk band The Vice. By that time, he was an ember of his former self. All his pep was gone. Punk was an easy route for him to take. He was able to shoot up and play profoundly for about an hour. It was scary how far he had fallen, from Broadway star to early-evening slots at CBs. The Vice could've harnessed his drug-fueled angst, but he couldn't even sustain that.

Brett bottomed out in the 90s, bouncing back and forth between New York and Florida. A series of petty crimes committed in the Sunshine State caught up with him. He got extradited from New York to Florida, where he ended up in the rehab unit of Broward County Jail.

Smiley got released from prison and began to rebuild his shattered life. He moved back in with his family in Brooklyn where he currently resides. He turned his negative experiences into a positive, and became an acting coach. Interest in him rekindled with 2003's indie release of the shelved *Breathlessly Brett* and 2005's Nina Antonia book *The Prettiest Star: Whatever Happened To Brett Smiley?*

Like many child stars, Smiley failed as an adult. His cherubic veneer of invincibility faded, his good looks evaporated, the lines on his face set deep, and the frustration of time ticked away. His promising career ended in tatters.

Brett Smiley surmised: "The whole androgyny thing was happening and I was particularly pretty. I grew up in the theater, and I was like this child star. So I was screwed up for life, I guess." ●

L-R: UK press photo, 1974; *Breathlessy Brett*, produced by Andrew Loog-Oldham, recorded 1975, released 2003; Brett Smiley biography, *The Prettiest Star*, by Nina Antonia, 2005. Photos by Gered Mankowitz. Courtesy of Brett Smiley.

  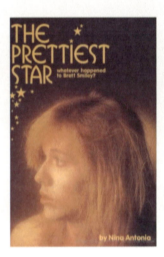

BETTY DAVIS

If I'm in luck, I just might get picked up
I said I'm vampin' trampin'—you can call
it what you wanna

— BETTY DAVIS, "IF I'M IN LUCK, I JUST MIGHT GET PICKED UP"

BETTY DAVIS (Betty O. Mabry) had what it takes to become a star, but something went wrong. She was born July 26, 1945 in Durham, North Carolina and grew up near Pittsburgh as a steelworker's daughter listening to her grandma's blues records. When she was 16, she moved to New York City to study apparel design at Fashion Institute of Technology. The lively 5'7" beauty was one of the first black Wilhelmina models, gracing covers of *Ebony*, *Glamour*, and *Seventeen*. In late 1966, Mabry went down to The Electric Circus and presented The Chambers Brothers with a tape of her first musical composition, "Uptown (To Harlem)." Their 1967 recording of that song signaled her arrival on the scene.

Her hot looks, musical chops, and eye for talent allowed her to ingratiate herself with famous stars of rock. She became a fixture at clubs, hobnobbing with a new breed that transcended race and included Jimi Hendrix and Sly Stone, who were drawn as much to her beauty as to her formidable musical acumen. She could talk music, and they responded to her with respect as an artist.

Mabry's modeling career kicked into high gear when she was chosen to appear on the cover of Miles Davis' 1968 album *Filles de Kilimanjaro*, on which he dedicated "Mademoiselle Mabry" to her. But Miles saw in her more than just a musical muse; he fell in love with her and married her while on tour in Gary, Indiana in September 1968. They stayed married for over a year, during which time she personally introduced the trumpet master to Jimi and Sly. Betty was half Miles' age—only 23—and was way too much for him. Her hip, young blackness coincided with Miles' reinvention on *Bitches Brew*. A project spearheaded by Betty that would've seen Miles and

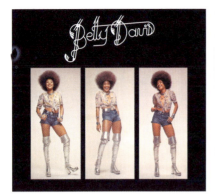

Above: Betty Davis album covers. L-R: *Betty Davis*, Just Sunshine Records, 1973. Photo by Mel Dixon; *Nasty Gal*, Island, 1975. Photo by Lorrie Sullivan; *Is It Love Or Desire*, 1976. Photo by Fin Costello. Courtesy of Light in the Attic Records.

Opposite top: Betty Davis fashion spread, *Rags* magazine, July 1970.
Opposite bottom: *Nasty Gal* publicity shoot, 1975. Photo by Charles Tracy.
Courtesy of Light in the Attic Records.

Jimi jam together did not happen because the latter did not read music as Miles required of all collaborators. Betty and Miles attended Jimi's funeral before their 1970 divorce over her alleged indiscretions with Hendrix and Hugh Masakela.

Gloria Jones recalls: "Betty Davis came to Hugh Masakela's recording session. This was the early 70s, when she used to wear shorts with Bermuda socks. We used to run into each other in the airport because we both traveled a lot in those days, and she'd always look fabulous. She and I would always take five or ten minutes to talk and encourage each other. She was really friendly, and we had this spiritual connection. She was a true artist. What I liked about Betty was she was not competitive, and was a true humanitarian. She was married to Miles, but stayed a humble girl from Pittsburgh."

Miles wrote in his autobiography, *Miles*: "Man, I was really in love again with Betty. She was young and really into new, avant-garde pop music. Betty was a big influence on my personal life as well as my musical life. She was just ahead of her time. She also helped me change the way I was

dressing. The marriage only lasted about a year, but that year was full of new things and surprises and helped point the way I was to go, both in my music and, in some ways, my lifestyle."

She developed her early-70s, Tina Turner-style, steamy funk (like "He Was a Big Freak" and "If I'm in Luck, I Just Might Get Picked Up"). It was cool, but it made minimal market impact despite world-class West Coast players such as Sly Stone rhythm section Larry Graham and Gregg Errico, Santana percussionist Michael Carabello, vocals by the Pointer Sisters, and horns by Tower of Power. 1973's *Betty Davis* and 1974's *They Say I'm Different* came out on Woodstock promoter Michael Lang's Just Sunshine label. Island issued 1975's *Nasty Gal* through a deal arranged by her new lover Robert Palmer. The cover art showed Betty in a red negligee, legs spread. She was an amazing performer with all the right skills and should've been huge, but nothing seemed to work out.

Betty Davis was on the verge of world-class stardom with her music and fashion hooks. But something terrible must have happened because she completely vanished from the public eye. Everyone that ever came out of Miles' circle became famous, so how is it the musician's wife didn't? Miles, on his 1981 *The Man With the Horn*, had three tunes about women in his life, including the metal-edged "Back Seat Betty."

It has been suggested that Betty Davis' retirement from music was less about personal failure and more due to revenge by a cuckolded ex-husband. Miles was a powerful and notoriously vengeful character, and she allegedly hurt him bad. But her raw sexuality was also at odds with 70s feminism and Christian activists. That resulted in nixed concerts, religious protests, and radio refusals. The NAACP derided her as a disgrace to her race! She was stunned by the cruelty and conservatism of the black status quo.

According to writer John Ballon, "When a popular Detroit radio station played 'If I'm in Luck, I Might Get Picked Up,' the lines lit up with outraged callers; a bomb threat followed. Within days, she was blacklisted by the NAACP."

She recounted, "Bourgeois blacks find me very offensive. They've been programmed to think that black women who shake their asses are whore-y. The NAACP called up the record company. They're trying to stop me from making a living. They stopped all my airplay in Detroit."

At the time of this writing, Betty Davis lives in anonymity, unreachable as if in hiding, in her suburban Pittsburgh hometown of Homestead. She seems almost embarrassed by her past: "I look back on those records, not so much as a reflection of myself, but as a representation of the time. It feels good to get recognized. In the end, the only advice I have is to be true to your art form. By that I mean do what's in your heart more than what's in your head." ●

"THIS SKIRT IS REALLY DIRTY"

"It's the way the star is done on the front; there are two more on the back. Hernando on 10th St. made it for me. I just wanted a nice little leather skirt with a star studded on it. I'm not really into short skirts, but if this had been long, it would have thrown the star off. The whole thing is in the star. I don't feel tough in it. I feel nice. It's nice to show your legs. The blouse is Mr. Freedom's, the belt by Ronnie Furst, the scarf from Betsey, Bunky & Nini and the boots from Bendel's."

PAT BRIGGS

I think I'm stuck, makin' no excuses and passin' the buck
Well I've just had twenty long years of real bad luck

— PSYCHOTICA, "ICE PLANET HELL"

PAT BRIGGS should have been a 90s rock star. He moved to New York in the mid-80s, where the charismatic, young, gay hustler took a bartending job at The Cat Club. There he sang in the glam-metal group R.U. Ready, equal parts Ziggy Stardust, Jane's Addiction, and Poison. *Billboard* reported the NYC scene sensation's signing as part of an RCA distribution deal. However the band's 1992 effort *R.U. Ready* was never released because the deal imploded. Briggs quit in disgust. Metal magazines of the day reported that he might replace Jani Lane as singer in Warrant, but that never came to be.

Briggs then took a job managing the club Don Hill's, where he co-founded Psychotica, a gender-bending goth/industrial group inspired by Klaus Nomi and Kabuki theater. Signed after their first rehearsal to Rick Rubin's American Recordings, the band was to be the next Marilyn Manson. They landed a spot touring with Lollapalooza, which should have been their gateway to bigger and better things. But Rubin detested 1996's *Psychotica*, despite production by Don Fury, logo design by Stephen Sprouse, and

a cover of DEVO's anthem "Freedom of Choice." After a year of ups and downs with Rubin, the band got dropped.

1998's *Espina* (Zero Hour), overseen by Nine Inch Nails producer Doug DiAngeles, featured a Psychotica with less of Briggs, more of guitarist Ena Kostabi (younger brother of artist Mark Kostabi) and cellist Enrique Tiru Velez. The album sported a redo of "MacArthur Park" (a hit for both Richard Harris and Donna Summer). 1999's *Pandemic* (Red Ant), a techno-ish jam Kostabi cut in an English castle (Great Lindford Manor in Milton Keynes), was rolled out at listening parties in New York and LA. But that record never got released because the Columbia-distributed label went out of business. So within seven years, three major labels dropped bands Briggs fronted.

From 1994 through 1999, Pat Briggs and Michael Schmidt (clothing designer for Cher and Michael Hutchence) hosted Squeezebox, a trashy, gay, rock and roll party for drag queens and straight onlookers at Don Hill's. Briggs disbanded Psychotica in order to start similarly themed

Patt Briggs, Hawaii, 2015. Selfie by Pat Briggs. Collection of Pat Briggs.

Pat Briggs, Psychotica, Don Hill's, New York, 1996. Collection of Pat Briggs.

clubs in Hollywood (Club Makeup) and Atlanta (Glitterdome), where he sang and toured with Georgia shock-rockers Impotent Sea Snakes. Briggs played the role of a gay musician in Alex Sichel's 1997 Riot Grrl film *All Over Me*, and spent 2001 at the bedside of terminally ill Carrie Hamilton, late daughter of Carol Burnett. Then he moved to Hawaii.

Briggs was well suited for stardom, being charismatic and good-looking. It was the era of Marilyn Manson, when appearing pansexual was a plus. He was theatrical and flamboyant and had the ingredients to be a household name, but this was a case where the strikes against the artist were rendered by outside forces.

There is no way to explain major label marketing; everything happens devoid of logic. Briggs was making records correctly but he was powerless in the face of arbitrary record label decision

making. He didn't really do anything wrong; through no fault of his own, his records went unreleased. He was worn down, less from music and art and more from industry one-upmanship and manipulation. It was not failure but rather perpetual limbo, which may be worse because with failure at least there is closure.

Pat Briggs reflects on his career: "When I was a child I was completely overlooked, disregarded and cast aside, and I vowed that when I grew up I would never let that happen again. This is now my 30th year in the entertainment business. And though I'm certainly not a household name, I'm still doing it, and doing it for the right reasons. I'm grateful to have the career I've had as a cult figure because most people never even get to taste that. I've been able to help a lot of people and make some miserable lives just a little brighter. And anyhow, the best is yet to come!" ●

BOBBY JAMESON

So many things to remember,
and so many more to forget
And all that I remember is all that
I'm trying to forget

— BOBBY JAMESON, "PLACES, TIMES AND THE PEOPLE"

BOBBY JAMESON never cared about school because he was destined to be a rock star. He flirted with early-60s teen idol fame, and then became a notorious LA hippie-counterculture musician, a peer of that era's most radical and volatile scenesters. Bobby's sound evolved through many phases, but he seemed most comfortable playing hard-driving country-rock.

There are many reasons you've never heard about Bobby: He was unable to cultivate an audience beyond record industry insiders and he lacked strong business advocates, so he got taken advantage of. Perhaps those evil music-biz sharks and wolves were to blame; perhaps he had no one to blame but himself.

Bobby was born April 20, 1945 in Geneva, Illinois near Chicago. He grew up in the Tucson, Arizona area, and moved around the Southwest during the 1950s. His mother suffered a series of failed marriages to cold, abusive male "role models." That flood of personal pain and lack of stability deeply affected Bobby.

"In 1958 my mother and stepfather separated and divorced. It was my mother's second failed marriage, and that was a very big loss for me. What little adult supervision I'd had became less. I was like a rudderless ship, struggling to find my way."

Bobby's grandmother was a concert violinist and his mother was musically inclined, so there was always music in the house. Bobby and his older brother Bill got swept up in the advent of rock and roll, watching *American Bandstand* and playing guitars bought at Sears. The sharply dressed siblings created an Everly Brothers-style act called The Macdonald Brothers (surname of a stepfather) that performed at school proms, sock hops, and talent shows.

The Macdonald Brothers won a talent search sponsored by Kal Rueben's Furniture City on Speedway Blvd. in downtown Tucson, resulting in the duo playing weekly from a podium on the store's main floor in an attempt to lure discount furniture shoppers. Bobby knew it was only a matter of time until he was bigger than Elvis Presley, Ricky Nelson, or Jerry Lee Lewis. He'd listen to the radio at night when he was supposed to be sleeping, memorizing the words to songs so that he could croon them the next day at school.

"As a kid I always felt out of place except when I was doing music. Music became an imperative because it was the one way I could escape not feeling loved or not feeling good enough—music always made me good enough. When I was in school, girls wouldn't pay attention to you, but if they knew you played music, they paid big attention. I was always broke, and music had the capacity to make people love you, to make people pay you, and make girls interested in you. There was a lot of motivation to go into music. In 1957 I knew what I was about to do with my life. I dreamed my way into the life I wanted, and I passed through my teen years with that focus."

Bobby and Billy experienced more than interest from the girls when the family moved to the hick town of St. Johns near Flagstaff. The brothers' rock star status resulted in enmity from redneck Mormon jocks and cowboys. It ended atrociously, at a school dance in which a fellow student confronted Bill and inflicted a savage beatdown. The traumatic episode caused

brain damage and mental and emotional issues from which Bill never recovered.

"People got envious of us after we performed at this high school assembly," Bobby explains. "These football players' girlfriends were suddenly eyeballing us, so they were jealous. We went to this school dance, and this one guy was a redneck yahoo Western-shirt type, very different than us. Somehow there was gonna be a fight. And my brother could fight good. So the whole dance ends up on the St. Johns High School's front lawn, including the principal. This guy sucker-punched my brother, so there wasn't a fight, and he went on to beat him as the white Mormon principal sat back and enjoyed the beating.

"It altered my life in many ways because my brother changed. He ended up in Arizona State Hospital in Phoenix because something inside of him broke. I remember the day he went in. He was 16 and I was 14 and these two guys dressed in white opened this big iron door and came and got him. I was standing there watching my brother go off to what was like a dungeon. This was like 1958, it was a bad place, and they closed that door and I remember that clank. They held him like a little rag doll, and that was the last time I saw him the way he was. He came out different after all the shock treatment they gave him.

"So I made up my mind to get away from all this, and music was the only possibility for a kid from Arizona that no one knew or gave a shit about. I knew I had this magic. I knew better than I've ever known anything in my life that I had this power, and that maybe with that I could take care of my brother. To me it was a very clear map of where I was going and why I had to go there, and there was nothing on this planet capable of altering my perception."

Bill and Bobby Jameson, Tucson, 1957. Collection of Bobby Jameson.

Bobby Jameson, his brother, and mother, Arizona, 1951. Collection of Bobby Jameson.

Come on everybody in the United States Come out to California because the surfin's great

— BOBBY JAMESON, "LET'S SURF"

IN 1962, BOBBY'S MOTHER fled yet another husband and moved again, this time far from the redneck hell of Arizona to the more sophisticated suburban-Los Angeles hamlet of Glendale, where Bobby attended Herbert Hoover High School.

"I got out of Arizona and went to California with my mother and brother," he recalls. "That Southwestern cowboy environment I'd come from hung on me like an ill-fitting jacket. It was obvious to people as soon as I began talking. So it became a training ground for reinventing myself, lock, stock, and barrel. I learned to talk different, walk different, and look different. I wanted to fit in and was ashamed I didn't. The last thing I wanted was for anyone to associate me with anything redneck, so I dressed like a surfer."

By the end of his senior year, 17-year-old Bobby spent most of his time in Hollywood, going to clubs and crashing with new friends, like guitarist Danny Whitten, bassist Billy Talbot, and drummer Ralph Molina. Those guys, from the Canton, Ohio doo-wop act Danny and the Memories, had recently moved to LA to record a single for Warner Brothers ("Can't Help Lovin' That Girl of Mine"). Years later, they came to fame as Neil Young's electric backup band, Crazy Horse.

"Hollywood was just over the hill, although it felt a million miles away. Whenever I got the chance, I'd go. I'd take the bus or if I got lucky, hitch a ride. It didn't matter how I got there. I knew that's where I was going to be, even though

Bobby Jameson, first
Talamo Records single,
"I'm So Lonely," 1964.
Collection of the author.

I wasn't there yet. I was going there because that's where they made records. That's where songs meant something. That's where the music business was. The place, in my mind, was the ultimate turn-on."

In 1963, the 18-year-old got his first shot at the music business, writing novelty surf songs for Louis Toscano's Jolum Records. That year Bobby cut his first single, "Let's Surf" b/w "Take This Lollypop." His name was wrongly printed on the label as "Bobby James." The Beach Boys-style 45 featured guitarist Elliot Ingber before his stints with The Mothers of Invention and Captain Beefheart. Bobby also wrote "California Surfer," the A-side to Jolum's 1963 single by 16-year-old female vocalist Dee D. Hope. Neither Toscano-produced release tore up the charts.

"I was always looking to sing for somebody," Bobby relates, "and there were these guys Kent Osborne and Louie Toscano. Some kid from Glendale they were trying to make into a pop star mentioned me to them. So we rode over on his motor scooter, and went to this house in Laurel Canyon where I smoked my first joint. It scared the crap out of me but I did it! I played them some music and they forgot about this other kid and got interested in me. They got this old guy to invest in a record. 'Let's Surf' was number-two in Truckee, California, but that was it. I was thinking my career was already over."

I'm as lonely as can be
Why won't she fall in love with me?

— BOBBY JAMESON, "I'M SO LONELY"

CAROLINA PINES WAS the struggling-artist coffee shop on Sunset Strip. It was there in early 1964 that Bobby, with his future Crazy Horse friends, met Tony Alamo, a hipster music promoter. Jameson expressed little interest when Alamo pitched to make him a star. But unlike most big talkers, Tony followed up his words by placing a series of ads featuring Bobby for his new label Talamo Records. The ads quickly grew over time from quarter-pagers to full-page and then elaborate pullouts in both *Billboard* and *Cashbox*, hailing Jameson as "The World's Next Phenomenon" and "The Star of the Century." There was no record and no music, and the ads showed a photo of Bobby in silhouette. Suddenly, the biz was abuzz about this ubiquitous new artist:

"In every picture his figure has been darkened so that it is not possible to make out his features. At this point the only thing I know for sure is that he plays a guitar. Whether or not Bobby Jameson will be a 'world phenomenon' is a question that only the future will answer. But in any event he has certainly been the subject of one of the slickest advertising campaigns of 1964."
— *Variety* (7/10/1964)

"That was my real introduction to the business," Bobby states. "I had no contract, no record, no anything. The Beatles were a 'phenomenon' so I was 'the next phenomenon.' Tony did this and never told me, it just happened. So the little kid who wants to be a star is now seeing Tony Alamo not as this blowhard but as the guy responsible for putting his name into the world's two biggest music trade papers. This man became the most important human being on the face of the planet to me because he was doing what I was dreaming about. This is how Tony set me up to follow his every command... Finally we had to go into the studio to make a record, so we recorded four songs, which I wrote, played, arranged, and produced. I got credit, but I never got paid a dime."

In April 1964 came "I'm So Lonely" b/w "I Wanna Love You," cut at Nashville West on Melrose Avenue. The Talamo single sold a reported 100,000 copies, and became a number-one hit in Cleveland and Detroit thanks to Windsor, Ontario's CKLW radio DJ Terry Knight, later the force behind 70s superstars Grand Funk. Via Terry and Tony, Bobby toured the Heartland as the opening act for The Beach Boys, Jan & Dean, and Chubby Checker. Three months later came the release of the swamp-blues stomp "Okey Fanokey Baby" b/w "Meadow Green." Jameson found out years later that Tony bootlegged his own records to sell at a discount to distributors, and that Alamo rejected major label offers for Bobby because it was more important for him to maintain control.

Bobby appeared on *American Bandstand* on September 26, doing "I'm So Lonely" and was interviewed by a young Dick Clark. But as luck would have it, his show was one of the few un-archived episodes, and has been lost to history. Jameson also played the song on the LA teen dance shows *9th Street West* and *The Lloyd Thaxton Show*, similarly never archived. (It was common in the 60s for broadcasters to save money on expensive tape by recording over previously aired shows.)

"I'll give Tony his credit," Jameson offers. "He could talk people into damn near anything. He sold Dick Clark on the idea because of the ads. I'm sure he lied about what he said he'd do, but he convinced Dick Clark to put me on *American Bandstand*. I used to watch the show and dream of being on it. All of a sudden I'm up there and all these kids were watching me. I looked good but I felt like a fragile piece of glass because I had no licks. I'm basically an amateur with this giant spotlight, and no way to cope."

Tony Alamo was a drifter con man, always trying to get money out of people. He never paid *Billboard* and *Cashbox* for those $15,000 in ads (the only person to ever pull off such a scam). Bobby will never forget one particular business meeting set up by Alamo: "We were in Beverly Hills, sitting at this 50-foot table with an old Jewish businessman smoking a cigar. Suddenly Tony stood up and shouted, 'That man is Bobby Jameson, and he is Jesus Christ. And if you don't give him $50,000, he will point his finger at

you and you will die!' And I sat there thinking, 'What the fuck is happening?' It was insanity. The cigar fell from the man's mouth. At that very moment I was terrified of Tony Alamo."

Alamo left music in the late 60s to become the charismatic leader of Tony Alamo Christian Ministries (infamous for leaflets left on the windows of parked cars). He is currently serving a 175-year sentence in the federal penitentiary outside of Terre Haute, Indiana on a range of child abuse charges. *Rolling Stone*, in a March 1972 feature on the cult/rock relation, delved into the Jameson/Alamo debacle:

"Tony became this Christian zealot out of nowhere," Jameson divulges, "and I was his focus. I was scared and I didn't know what he'd do next... He gave me my first upper, a Dexedrine, because I was exhausted. He said, 'You've got a show to do.' I remember he took out a little bottle, and within about 30 minutes I was so amped up, I did a show that got me a standing ovation! Then I got into that cycle where it was alcohol to come down, uppers to go up. I never knew where I was or what was going on, I was exhausted and I kept doing it for months. I went from a nobody to a somebody in weeks."

Bobby Jameson, various *Billboard* and *Cashbox* ads, 1964. Collection of Bobby Jameson.

Every place I go always reminds me All the times we had are now behind me

— BOBBY JAMESON, "ALL I WANT IS MY BABY"

DURING HIS TALAMO DAYS, Bobby received a letter from Andrew Loog Oldham, producer of the Rolling Stones (who hadn't yet toured the States). In his letter, Oldham raved about Jameson's vocal talents and offered to work together if the aspiring star ever went to London. Bobby spoke about the letter to his friend Peter Caine, photographer of the aforementioned Talamo ads. He in turn reached Lee Karsian of Ashley Famous Artists to see what could be done. Karsian verified Oldham's offer, and within weeks the three flew to London.

"All of a sudden, I had a reason to get away from Tony," Bobby recalls. "Everything moved real fast, and I could never get situated. Within a day or so in London we were going to meet Mick Jagger in the studio. They were all treating me like I'm somebody, I'm trying to convince them the Stones were big in America, and they did not believe me."

On November 27, 1964, Oldham produced Bobby's single, the Keith Richard penned song "All I Want Is My Baby" b/w Mick Jagger's "Each And Every Day" released on Decca UK. The session included Mick and Andrew on backup vocals, Keith as "music director," and a pre-Led Zeppelin Jimmy Page on guitar. Almost everyone was thrilled with the results.

"So then we go into the studio, and Andrew and Mick were having this exchange and they were like two raving queens. They presented me with 'All I Want Is My Baby.' Andrew tells the engineer to play the song, and I'm standing there, listening to this bad version of a Phil Spector-style song with a great fuzztone guitar. Then Andrew gets out this piece of paper and says, 'These are the lyrics. I want you to try and sing it.' I said, 'Well, I've got some songs.' And he says, 'I'm not interested.' I asked again if we could try my material and he was vehement, saying, 'No, we're gonna do this.' Two takes later, that was the record. I figured we were just rehearsing. I never spoke to Andrew again."

The young American made for perfect British pop-machine fodder with his newly bought Carnaby Street threads, proto-Beatles haircut, and sexy good looks. Despite his estrangement with Oldham, Bobby became a bona fide star across the pond, sipping wine with The Beatles at The Ad Lib club in West London, and making the scene with his Rolling Stones cache. When the single came out, it received impressive press. It was heavily promoted, with splashy ads and pushy publicists, included in a feature in January 1965's issue of *Vanity Fair* (UK) photographed by a young Richard Avedon, and an article the next month in the British Invasion hot-sheet *Fab*.

"I gotta give it to Decca," Bobby concedes, "They promoted the crap out of it. I was this American pop star in the British papers but at the same time I was a kid from Arizona trying to figure out what just happened. Here I was living in London like a little prince, a little king, with a nice apartment in the aristocratic Belgravia area. That photo from *Fab* was shot there, and back then I really did look like one of The Beatles."

December 16, 1964, Jameson performed on *Ready Steady Go*, the biggest British teen pop TV show at the time. It was a disaster. He forgot the lyrics he was supposed to be lip-syncing. Because of the negative feedback, he decided in press interviews to air his criticisms of "All I Want Is My Baby." Needless to say, his "ins" with the Stones soured. He quickly began to earn a reputation as an agitator and a weak asset, especially after the single's lack of success.

"All of a sudden I do this TV show," he recounts, "and it's huge and it's live, aired to the entire British Isles. I didn't really know what I was doing. I didn't like the record so I hadn't been tightening up on it to lip-sync it properly. I just didn't want to do it. So I get there and they had a dumb-looking set with tinker-toys and paper-wood fences. Then I missed a producer cue at the song's opening. I never saw the show, but in my estimation it was a travesty. I was really upset by it all. Everyone involved in my record thought that they were going to become a millionaire because if Andrew Loog Oldham was involved, then it was a sure thing. But I never got a penny, not then, not now, not ever."

Keith Richards, in his autobiography, derided Jameson as "P.J. Proby's valet" (a reference to Bobby's friend, another 60s almost-rock-star). Richards' invective was in response to Bobby's anti-Stones remarks on the web. To that Bobby retorted in a 2012 blog entry: "The problem that I have with Richards' remark is I was never paid for doing this record. It was put out as a single worldwide on Decca and London Records, and can be found on multiple albums of Rolling Stones-involved work since 1964. In the last 45 years I haven't gotten anything for it, so it seems belittling to me at this point, after I already got fucked over by Oldham, Richards, Jagger, Decca, and whoever else has had anything to do with the record. It's a little pathetic. If you're going to badmouth another artist I'd suggest it not be one that you screwed out of money."

In early 1965, Bobby rebuffed overtures from the hippie managers of The Pretty Things because he wanted to be represented by someone powerful and dressed in a suit. So he signed to Brit Records, owned by a young Chris Blackwell (prior to his founding of Island Records), who had just had a hit with Millie Smalls' "My Boy Lollipop" and was seeking new artists. Jameson made a single with producer Harry Robinson called "Rum Pum (Mum Num)," a novelty song with nursery rhyme-like lyrics that Jameson wrote three years earlier and that had been covered by Tommy Roe of "Dizzy" fame (without recompense to Bobby). The single, "cut live with half of the London Philharmonic" and heralded on the front cover of one of the first issues of *New Musical Express*, also failed to gain traction.

"My music was going to a heavier, deeper place," Bobby says, "and everyone was trying to keep me as this shallow pop star. So I was rejecting it as I was doing it. I had these opportunities but I sabotaged it all at the same time."

May 1, 1965 was the beginning of Bobby's end in London. He enraged TV producers of *Thank Your Lucky Stars* when he did not wear his "trademark" black leather glove on his right hand, after the London papers had all just written about "the glove." He did so after a hash-stoned backstage dare by Dylan producer John Hammond. Chris Blackwell was angry and quit on Jameson, as did the rest of his handlers. P.J. Proby had once told him, "You'll know when it's time to leave England…" So with no money and nowhere to turn, Bobby pled his case to the American Consulate. Days later, he was on a one-way flight home.

"I was still 19 and I'm in a foreign country, and everybody walked out," he maintains. "The

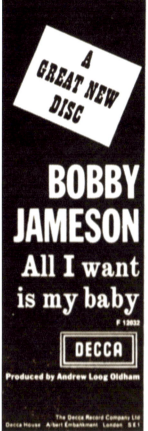

apartment lease had another month, so I was there alone with no money, no nothing, and I freaked out. I didn't know what to do. I was an abandoned child in essence. I had been a big deal and now I felt like a total failure as this whole thing went into the shitter. In one year I had been on two British labels, but I was like this curiosity, this oddball. But I never got over the hump, so to speak, although I got close. I was Mister Almost-Success. I wanted to go back to America and then nobody would help me leave. It was all real fast: pop star, pop star, pop star, and then nothing. When it was time to go, there was nobody to say good-bye to. All I had was $20 in my pocket, my guitar case, and suitcase."

Jameson arrived in Los Angeles and took the bus to Ben Frank's, the Sunset Strip rock-and-roll eatery. He arrived there without enough money for a meal. As he walked in, he saw a woman he vaguely remembered who offered him a couch to crash on. "I spent the next 20 years living like that on people's couches. There were some nice couches," Jameson jokes. "I stayed alive because of moments like that."

"It was 1965 and the psychedelic thing was starting to pop. It was a new feeling. I left America and it was one way, and when I got back a year and a half later, it was another. It went from that red-velvet, pointed-shoes and slicked-back hair to flower child. There was the British Invasion, and the American response with The Byrds and Buffalo Springfield just coming into play. So I went out and started to mingle on the Sunset Strip because that was the place. People were responsive and interested in each other. It was the start of the hippie movement. It was amazing. It was an energy you can't explain unless you were there. It was different than anything that had ever happened. It just kind of lifted you. And I was there right at the beginning of it."

1964 was almost the year of Bobby Jameson. Top: Talamo Records ad for April 1964's "I'm So Lonely" and July 1964's "I Wanna Love You" singles. Bottom: Decca UK ad for November 1964's "All I Want Is My Baby," produced by Andrew Loog Oldham and written by Keith Richards. Collection of Bobby Jameson.

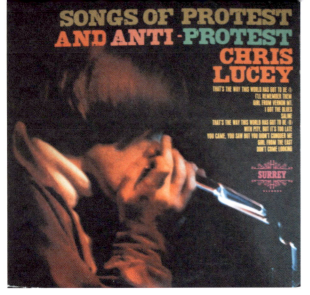

Too many feelings of sorrow and grief
Too many feelings of complete disbelief

— CHRIS LUCEY, "THAT'S THE WAY THE WORLD'S GOT TO BE (PT. 2)"

THEN, IN A BIZARRE EPISODE, Jameson made a record under the name Chris Lucey. It was Mira Records' convoluted attempt to resurrect an album cancelled at the last minute by a musician named Chris Ducey. During his late-night Sunset Strip activities Bobby got cozy with Pam Burns, the assistant to Mira president Randy Woods, who'd recently left Vee Jay after fame as Pat Boone's producer. Pam presented Bobby as a possible stand-in for this record on Mira's sub-imprint, Surrey.

"Surrey Records was kind of a budget line for Europe," Bobby recalls. "It was a rack job operation sold on the visual interest of shoppers from metal racks at grocery, drug, and variety stores for discount prices. They had an album by Chris Ducey that they had issues with due to a contract dispute. What they did was take the original Chris Ducey album cover, and they took out part of the 'D' on the printing press so it was now an 'L.' So the person would be Chris Lucey and the songs didn't exist except for the titles on the cover, and I was asked to

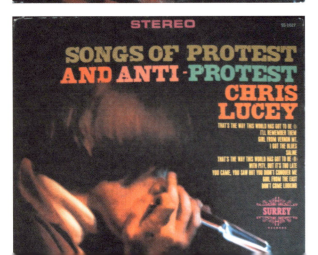

Bobby Jameson, his album as Chris Lucey also released as Chris Ducey, *Songs of Protest and Anti-Protest*, Surrey, 1965. Collection of Bobby Jameson.

write new songs with the existing titles. No one else wanted the job. But I was broke, so I took their $200 in expenses and said, 'I can do that.' It wasn't like they offered me a contract or respected me as an artist. There was no talk of publishing or a recording contract. They didn't give a shit about me, but they knew I could do it."

Marshall Leib, relatively famous as a member of Phil Spector's first band The Teddy Bears, produced 1965's *Songs of Protest and Anti-Protest* by Chris Lucey. Ironically, the LP's front cover photo was of the Stones' Brian Jones playing live at The Action Club in LA. Bobby wrote all the record's songs—a 60s mish-mash of jazz, folk-rock, and blues—except for "That's the Way the World's Got to Be (Part 2)" by recovering brother Bill Jameson. The album garnered minimal press response or radio airplay, and descended into musical oblivion. The late Leib told the *Los Angeles Herald-Examiner* (4/3/74): "I was supposed to be producing Chris Ducey. The new singer, I did not care for him or his music and I didn't want to do it. But the record sounded better than I thought."

The European release started to sell, so Mira issued the album as *Too Many Mornings* by Bobby Jameson for Canada. Then they released it as *Bobby Jameson* on Crestview, another division of Mira. Then there were a few "Chris Lucey" records sold in original, unaltered Chris Ducey covers. The record was also part of a Vee Jay Records box set. Mirwood Music, Pobleri Music, and Valentine Music, all ventures of Randy Woods' partner Betty Ciappetta, have claimed Bobby's Chris Lucey publishing. Ciappetta sold the UK master to Ace Records, who licensed it to Cherry Red, who leased it to Revola Music. So there are six versions of that record, and Bobby says he never got paid other than the initial $200. (The real Chris Ducey's next group, Penny Arkade, produced by The Monkees' Michael Nesmith, never got off the ground.)

"They weren't interested in what was in it musically, Ducey's version or mine," Bobby stresses. "They loved the album jacket's artwork and the Brian Jones photo. They knew it would sell on sight… But the response was so poor that I was embarrassed. I'd try to go up to people and say, 'Here's my new album' and they'd say 'Hey, that doesn't look like you.' And I'd say, 'No, that's Brian Jones.' Then they'd say 'Well, who's Chris Lucey?' And I'd say, 'I am.' I had this album with someone else's picture and someone else's name. I tried to promote the record but finally I just said 'screw it.' It was a mess."

Later that year, Jameson suffered an unsettling physical attack by Randy Woods over his refusal to sign a contract on the Chris Lucey album, a contract that offered no additional money. Bobby was particularly distrustful of any legal paperwork written by Randy's cutthroat attorney Abe Somer (later notorious as manager of Three Dog Night). Jameson contends the record was put out illegally because there was no artist contract or publishing deal.

"I'm 20 years old and I have zero representation and nobody on my side, and they want me to sign this contract. So I say, 'Well, what do I get?' And Randy Woods flips out and threw me up against the friggin' wall. He got right in my face and said, 'You little son of a bitch!' So I said, 'I ain't signing the contract.' At some point they let me out of the office but I never signed their deal. Randy realized he'd physically assaulted me, and the whole office knew it. I guess someone spoke to him, saying, 'You committed a crime in essence against Bobby, physically manhandling him.' He decided he'd let me make a single, any single I wanted. So I said 'okay' and wrote 'Vietnam.'"

Said I got a call from Uncle Sam Said 'send that boy to Vietnam'

— BOBBY JAMESON, "VIETNAM"

"VIETNAM," JAMESON'S 1966 SINGLE, was released right after the U.S. Army announced its Vietnam War draft. The fiery anti-war paean, written after he received his draft notice (later deferred for mental issues) came out on Mira but was not promoted due to its politics. Members of Mira labelmates The Leaves supplied a Bo Diddley backbeat to his harmonica-laden howl. The garage rockers had recently recorded Bobby's "Girl from the East" from the Chris Lucey LP as the flipside to their version of "Hey Joe" (later reworked into a hit by Jimi Hendrix). Drummer Don Conka of Arthur Lee and Love played on the session. That backing band also excelled on the B-side's acid-rock nugget "Metropolitan Man."

Phil Turetsky—Randy Woods' crony, Johnny Rivers' business manager, and Pacific Jazz Records president—also played a role in the Jameson saga. Through Phil, "Vietnam" and "Metropolitan Man" were used in 1967's cult film *Mondo Hollywood*. Turetsky's friend, director Robert Carl Cohen, wrote in the soundtrack's liner notes that Bobby "became part of *Mondo* by fulfilling one or more of the three criteria: 1. Be typically Hollywood (i.e. trying to live out a dream self-image in the LA area) 2. Or be very weird. Or 3. be both 1 and 2."

British rock journalist Jon Savage recently wrote, "In the pantheon of protest, Bobby Jameson's 'Vietnam' is not well known but it is both early and extremely effective—with its deep level bass rumble and totally committed vocal. It comes off as a blast of—if not exactly blue-collar, then at least suburban—rage." (*The Guardian*, 11/10/10).

Jameson escaped the clutches of Randy Woods by signing a deal with the Hollywood-based Current Records. That label was run by Crusader Records' producer John Fisher (an LA promoter noted for his own minor hit as Johnny Fisher, 1960's "Tell Me Yes") and one Mike Goldberg. 1965's "All Alone" b/w "Your Sweet Loving" single, a bluesy Stones-ish gem with Bobby credited as writer and arranger, got recorded in an afternoon. But it was never promoted, and faded quickly. Soon after, Bobby stormed into Goldberg's office, demanding answers. Mike had a story about LA radio not responding to the record, and that there was absolutely nothing he could do about it.

Jameson still cringes over that disaster: "That was a good record on Current, and no one even knew it. I was so pissed off, I couldn't see straight. This guy sweet-talked me into signing the goddamn thing and now he wanted money to buy myself out of a deal because he didn't do his job promoting the record. It was only $500 or $600 to reimburse the full cost of the session, but for me that was a lot. So I conned this woman infatuated with me named Carol Paulus, who I still know, to buy my way out of that contract."

April 22, 1967   THE BEAT   Page 11

...THEN...NOW...WHENEVER!!!

Bobby Jameson,
KRLA *The Beat*,
April 22, 1967.
Collection of
Bobby Jameson.

Walkin' down the highway in my highway shoes I don't know where I'm going, got nothin' to lose

— BOBBY JAMESON, "GOTTA FIND MY ROOGALATOR"

RANDY WOODS CAME BACK into the picture as the distributor of the Pat Boone-connected Penthouse Records. The label was the music industry foray of Mattel Toys heir Ken Handler (the inspiration for the Ken doll). Jameson made two singles for Penthouse. December 1965's "Reconsider Baby" was his response to Percy Sledge's "When a Man Loves a Woman." The title of September 1966's "Gotta Find My Roogalator" contained a funky synonym for "mojo" that Bobby picked up from motorcycling with Johnny Rivers, Johnny on his 750 Triumph and Bobby on a 650 BSA.

Bobby used to run into a young Frank Zappa at the love-ins, and the two freaks hit it off. Bobby hired Frank to arrange and play guitar on both Penthouse singles, but Zappa received no credit on the first. Other players on those recordings went on to become the famed LA session squad The Wrecking Crew. Handler's partner Norm Ratner took credit as the producer but Jameson and Zappa did all the work.

Bobby recalls how his Penthouse deal ended: "Both those records were neither promoted nor distributed worth a crap by Penthouse for a reason. Ken Handler was gay. He was married

Bobby Jameson, *Rolling Stone* feature by Judith Sims, October 26, 1972. Photo by Richard Creamer. Collection of Bobby Jameson.

but he way gay. He treated me like a star, buying me guitars and a motorcycle. One night, I was invited to his house in Woodland Hills. As his wife cooked dinner downstairs he brought me upstairs to his office. He said, 'I'd like you to spend the night here with me.' And I said, 'Well, I'm not up for that, Ken.' He was pretty cool about it all but he said, 'Is that your final position?' When I told him yes, he said, 'Well that's too bad because my interest in you was directly hinged on this question.'

"So he made me return all this gear. When he asked for the 650 BSA bike, I refused. I said, 'I'm keeping that, I earned it.' If I would've slept with him I could've been a pop star, but I wouldn't so I was out... Here I was having made 'Vietnam,' 'All Alone,' 'Reconsider Baby' and 'Roogalator'—three labels and four records since Chris Lucey, in less than two years. And I still had no money. I was back in the same place, and in the same situation, trying to make money off of music, and I got zip for all of it."

Bobby's bit in *Mondo Hollywood* played a significant role in Frank Zappa's history. In his brief scene, Jameson walks on the beach with his then-girlfriend Gail Sloatman, a lovely cocktail waitress he met at the Sunset Strip hippie club The Trip. Gail came along with Bobby when he visited Frank. She later became Gail Zappa, mother of Dweezil, Ahmet, Moon Unit, and Diva.

"It was 1966 and we started hanging out, boyfriend-girlfriend. I started going up to Zappa's first place in Laurel Canyon by the country store, and I'd take Gail with me. And Frank was making a movie shooting these miniature figures on his dining room table, and I was sitting on his floor writing songs for my next album as he did that. Gail was living with me up at the house off Woodrow Wilson Drive where all the LSD was being sold. I wasn't a dealer; I just wanted to be closer to the source.

"One day Frank says to me, 'I've got a got a problem, we need to speak about Gail.' I said, 'What's wrong, is she bothering you?' He said, 'No, I just really want to know how interested you were in her because I care about her but I don't want to do anything to negatively affect our friendship.' I said, 'Hey no worries. I'm not bothered. If you like each other, go for it.' He seemed relieved and that was all that was ever said about it."

Gail Zappa, in a 1994 interview with George Petros (*Seconds*, #41), told a different story of her meeting Frank: "I was the secretary for the guy who owned The Whiskey, Elmer Valentine. There was another girl who worked in the office part-time and did filing. I went to her house for dinner and, coincidentally, she shared a house with Frank. He called that evening and said, 'I'm at the airport. Come and get me—and don't bring anyone.' Of course she disobeyed and brought me. I met him at Los Angeles Airport."

You said you loved me baby, you said you would be true
Now you're running around all over town with every boy, what can I do?

— BOBBY JAMESON, "ALL ALONE"

IN THE SUMMER OF 1965, Phil Turetsky got Bobby an audition for a role in *The Monkees*. Jameson was strongly considered for the gig, though he troubled the show's creators Burt Schneider and Bob Raphelson by expressing artistic ambitions for the group. Eventually Bobby turned down the offer because he wanted to do a solo album with engineer Steve Clark and producer Curt Boettcher (behind The Association's sunshine-pop hits "Cherish" and "Along Comes Mary"), who Phil had introduced to Bobby.

"Phil was a very hip guy, even though he wore these tweed suits. He was very laid back. He'd been watching this fiasco go on with me, and decided he wanted to intervene because he thought I was talented and that everything that had gone on was nonsense. He told me of this TV pilot *The Monkees*, like an American version of *A Hard Day's Night*. He thought I'd be perfect for it. We arrived at Columbia Studios on Gower Street in Hollywood. I met Raphelson and Schneider and then Davy Jones, who had already been chosen as the first Monkee. They were all real nice and excited to meet me. It was a very positive experience. But I was starting to grow my hair and a beard for the first time, and they said I needed a haircut. Then I asked if the show was going to be as hip as *A Hard Day's Night*, and they assured me it would be that hip. But from the beginning I got the feeling that it was going to be exactly the way it turned out to be: kind of lame."

Frank Zappa introduced Verve Records' Tom Wilson to Bobby. Wilson, an African-American Harvard graduate, had recently produced albums by The Mothers of Invention and The Velvet Underground. Wilson dug the Curt Boettcher connection, so in March 1967 Verve released *Color Him In* under the moniker "Jameson." The cover art to this lost psych-rock classic left a section of Bobby's face unprinted, so that one could "color him in," like a children's coloring book.

"*The Monkees* and *Color Him In* came at the same time, through Phil Turetsky, but they went in different directions. One, I was going to have the freedom to decide what I wanted to cut. The other, I was going to be a Monkee and do what I was told. I met with Clark and Boettcher and played them the songs I wrote on Frank's floor. They loved it and everything was *kumbaya*. When Steve offered me $100 a week to write songs, I passed on *The Monkees* to work with them. I assume Frank felt indebted to me for his wife, and got Tom Wilson to get Verve to buy the album from the production company of Steve and Curt. There was a $10,000 check for me, that Steve talked me into signing over to him, and then he used my money to pay me my $100 a week!"

The record flopped. Subsequently, Bobby demoed five new songs on November 2, 1967 at Harmony Recorders on Melrose Avenue with Steve Clark at the controls. Songs included the dark, autobiographical "Born to Be a Loser" and the histrionic "The Death of a Lamb." That session resulted in Verve cutting ties with Jameson.

1968's *Working* album was also made with Steve Clark at Harmony Recorders, funded by studio owner Bob Ross. The LP featured versions of The Band's "The Weight," The Beatles' "Norwegian Wood," and Glen Campbell's "Gentle on My Mind." Solid players such as Elvis Presley sidemen James Burton and Jerry Scheff contributed. The poorly received effort came out on GRT (General Recorded Tape), a California-based tape manufacturer that went into the record business. Bobby still seethes while discussing what would be his final full-length release: "People are always saying to me, 'What are you so pissed off for?' I'm pissed off 'cause I got ripped off. I never got paid for anything in my entire life. And when I got paid, I just got paid back money I spent to get it made."

Bobby was the original king of the Sunset Strip. He got deep into drugs, mainly heroin and LSD. He devolved into a dangerous man, arrested 27 times and declared dead from ODs twice. The press wrongly tied him to his friend Diane Linkletter's suicide leap from her sixth-floor window of the Shoreham Towers in October 1969. His name also arose during that summer's LAPD inquiry into the Manson murders after he and two others got busted in Benedict Canyon on an unrelated grand theft auto charge.

He also nearly drank himself to death, guzzling a half-gallon of rotgut scotch a day, a talent he developed while trying to kick a barbiturate habit. Years of depravity, plus all his unmet hopes and cyclical failures coupled with the news of his estranged father's suicide, resulted in him spending time at Edgemont Hospital on Hollywood Blvd. on suicide watch.

"The more I thought about all the things that happened to me, the more it affected me, and

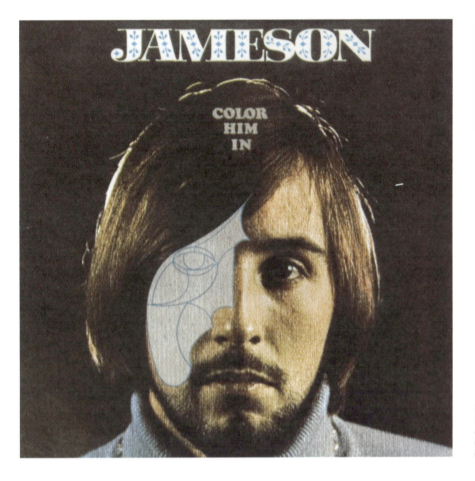

Front cover of Jameson, Verve, 1967, along with back cover, inset. Cover and design by George S. Whiteman. Collection of Bobby Jameson.

pissed me off. When Randy Woods threw me against the wall in 1965, I swore that no one would ever lay their hands on me again in this fucking industry, and if they did I'd kick the shit out of them. I was 20 years old then, and that promise was kept. I became well known as a bar fighter and street brawler; I had some big time fights in Beverly Hills at posh places. But I was interesting enough that people allowed me to keep coming. I was being treated like a celebrity on one hand and a deadbeat on the other, simultaneously. I became famous for who I dated, who married who I dated, and people I had worked with. But I was more famous in the long run for being a crazy son of a bitch, and basically I slowly went crazy, the kind of crazy that happens from too much drugs, alcohol, frustration, and struggle. I had a beautiful girlfriend, a Playboy Bunny, that I had to make leave me because she was loyal and I didn't want her to follow me to Hell."

Bobby Jameson, as Robert Parker Jameson, RCA Records promotional photo, 1978. Collection of Bobby Jameson.

If you want to move a little Come on down and bring your country fiddle

— BOBBY JAMESON, "GOOD OLE MUSIC"

BOBBY'S MUSIC MORPHED into a fusion of heavy rock and redneck-rebel attitude in sync with the rise of "country rock." His old friends Danny Whitten, Billy Talbot, and Ralph Molina, fresh off an album as The Rockets, checked Jameson out of Edgemont on a day pass in 1969 to cut four songs of tweaked Americana. The tunes, never released, included some of Bobby's finest work. "Big Spoke Wheel" featured pedal steel guitar legend Red Rhodes and LA session superstar Gib Guilbeau on fiddle.

From 1971–1973, Jameson played rootsy music and took hard drugs with Jesse Ed Davis, the late, Oklahoma-bred, Native American, ex-Conway Twitty guitarist (who'd just made a star-studded eponymous solo album for Atco that featured Gram Parsons and Eric Clapton). A young Randy Newman played piano on the duo's songs "Junkie Jesus" and "Jesus Was an Outlaw, Too." Some of the music, recorded on a MGM soundstage in Culver City, served as background in the 1971 film

Clay Pigeons with Telly Savalas and Robert Vaughn. While on a 1975 U.S. tour as the second guitarist for The Faces, Jesse Ed Davis, interviewed for his hometown paper *The Norman Transcript* before the band's show in Oklahoma City, stated: "I recently made some of my best music with this singer Bobby Jameson. That guy is something else. He should be way more popular than he is."

Bobby moved to Cleveland to work with a Blood, Sweat & Tears-style, brass-heavy rock group called Rastus. They had a farmhouse in nearby Chardin, Ohio. He credits his days spent in rural seclusion for saving his life: "I went to GRT to beg for some money, and they flat-out said no. But this guy there John Rhys, who produced Rastus, offered to take me to Cleveland to write songs for them and carry their equipment. I needed to leave LA because there was death around me, and I knew I was gonna die because I looked like shit and just shaved my head and was demoralized on every level. I jumped from a 12-story radio tower on Hollywood Boulevard and broke multiple bones."

Needless to say, the Rastus thing didn't work out. Jameson entered into a toxic junkie relationship with a new girlfriend. Eventually the two turned to AA. At that point, her rich investment-banker father contributed heavily to Bobby's career, because of his belief in the singer's talents, and to give his daughter a job in artist management. The singer explains the irony: "I was 31 years old in 1976, and had been making records and writing songs professionally since 1963. His first $15,000 check was more money than I'd made the entire time I'd been in the music business."

Bobby allocated some of that money to cut a demo in October 1976 at Wally Heider's Studio B in Hollywood, backed by members of Steely Dan and Toto. Guitar star Steve Lukather's slick licks are all over the tunes, which were written and produced by Jameson with Ben Benay, who'd worked on *Color Him In* and *Working*.

RCA liked the new demo and signed Bobby in early 1977. They put out a 1978 single under his full name Robert Parker Jameson. Bobby said he used his full name "because I wanted to disconnect from the past and what I perceived as my failures." The single, "Stay With Me" b/w "Long Hard Road," showed promise with airplay in Cleveland and New Jersey and across New England. For a moment, things looked promising for Bobby.

But that relationship soured after a few run-ins with RCA president Bob Summers. Among the issues was Jameson's refusal to hire Summers' friend, a notorious Nashville coke dealer, as manager. Other problems arose from Bobby's visit to the RCA warehouse in Cleveland, to see why no one could find his record, and discovered only 12 copies in stock. In the end, an unhappy RCA put the kibosh on a planned Robert Parker Jameson album.

"RCA never did ship records to the markets where radio airplay created a demand," Bobby wrote in 1999. "Whether by stupidity or purposeful sabotage, 'Stay With Me' was left hanging on the tree to rot in the sun. In time it fell to the ground and was left for dead, while my girlfriend and I and her family were left to bury the carcass. My positive demeanor was again ripped away by circumstances, and replaced with that old familiar failure persona. My stable 'can do' attitude of the past few years disappeared under the bright lights of humiliation. As I struggled to maintain not only my sobriety but my sanity during this chaos, I am stricken, even now, by the enormity of that dismal task. Day after day, month after month, I disintegrated into a familiar terrain of Bobby Jameson, 'loser.'"

Bobby Jameson, home in San Luis Obispo, CA, 2009. Collection of Bobby Jameson.

You cling to your money and think it's kind of funny
While others stand starving and alone

— BOBBY JAMESON, "METROPOLITAN MAN"

BOBBY RETIRED FROM MUSIC in 1985 to deal with his resurgent substance abuse. At the time of this writing, he lives in a trailer-park home outside of San Luis Obispo, where he works as a day laborer doing odd jobs, and spends much of his time detailing his professional travails on the Internet.

In 2010, the band Brian Jonestown Massacre released a version of Bobby's "There's a War Going On." Jameson said that he was given some money and was then asked to sign some murky paper-work, which he refused to do. Indeed, the more things change the more they stay the same. Bobby's neighbor told us, "I had no idea he was almost a rock star. I will now look at him differently. He's the guy you hire to clear your tree stumps."

Bobby Jameson may not have been the greatest singer or songwriter. But his career was consistently undermined and manipulated by shifty managers and record execs either neglecting to pay him, issuing his music without full legal approval, or subjecting him to outright physical, sexual, and psychological misconduct. And as in the broken home he longed to escape, he never got the attention or recognition he so craved.

"My addiction to wanting to be famous and successful was the major driving force. It blinded me. I was determined to be a star, and it was an addiction worse than heroin and booze and crack put together. It's unrelenting; it has no capacity not to see itself as accomplished."

Is this heaven, is this hell or am I just lost
Forever the junkie son of God on the cross

— BOBBY JAMESON, "JUNKIE JESUS"

BOBBY HAS COME TO UNDERSTAND that his negative outlook largely results from his years of bitter experiences in the music business, and that the pain of those setbacks factored into his avalanche of poor choices and inappropriate behavior. He was young and naive and overly trusting, and got burned for that. A few kept promises and adequate paychecks could have made a world of difference to his career trajectory.

"How do I feel about it?" he asks rhetorically. "I say don't fuck with me because I'm like Doc Holliday. He was a skinny, sick, dangerous fucker, and that is who I am. The Tony Alamos, the Randy Woods, the Steve Clarks, and the Andrew Oldhams—they took a nice kid who played songs and raped him repeatedly. If they took nothing it wouldn't matter. But they gained in some way and I got nothing, and that's wrong. They just threw me away."

Bobby has a particularly sad story from the 1980s of getting thrown out of the ASCAP building for trying to collect unpaid royalties. He was told there was a significant amount of money listed in his name but that he'd need to pursue the case legally. To date, he has been unable to get it together to find a lawyer to take his convoluted case on a pro bono basis. His "open letters" to ASCAP president Paul Williams have been met with silence. This writer's call to ASCAP to verify Jameson's story received no reply.

"I wrote song after song after song after song after song. Everything was going wrong and I felt like 'I am the most worthless piece of crap.' You can't have this much bad luck and be this full of shit. I said, 'Yeah you can, if you're name's Bobby Jameson.' For all I've done, I've got nothing to show for it. I don't have a nice home or a comfortable life. There's no happiness in my life. There's no peace in my life. There's just hardcore 'I can survive anything because I'm Bobby Jameson.'" ●

RIK FOX

LR009

Bitter streets of evil stares
No one listens, no one cares

— STEELER, "COLD DAY IN HELL"

RIK FOX (Richard Suligowski) is an overlooked hero of hair metal. He was born December 28, 1955 in Amityville, Long Island and raised in the Polish-American neighborhood of Greenpoint, Brooklyn. Before he started playing music, he photographed New York glam-rock groups like The Brats, The Planets, and KISS. Contemplating his portraitures helped him create a look for his own bands. Fox's musical debut was with The Martian Rock Band, who played CBGB and Max's Kansas City circa 1975. In 1976, he joined a top New Jersey glam-rock cover band called Virgin, later rebranded SIN. In 1981 he played bass with tri-state club stars The E. Walker Band. But Fox was preparing for bigger and better things.

At the invitation of Blackie Lawless, Fox moved to LA and for four months was in the original lineup of Blackie's band Sister. Fox came up with a cooler name for that band: W.A.S.P. But personal conflicts and the usual bullshit drove him from that band. He then played in Ron Keel's Sunset Strip sensation Steeler (which launched guitar god Yngwie Malmsteen). He played on 1983's *Steeler* for producer Mike Varney's Shrapnel label. *Steeler* went on to be the highest-selling independent metal LP at that time. His bandmates smelled money and launched solo careers, leaving Fox high and

dry. W.A.S.P. and Steeler were two of the most important bands in LA metal history, yet Fox remains little more than a footnote.

By the mid 80s, a newly resurrected LA lineup of SIN featured Fox alongside former members of the Long Island band Alien, including singer Frank C. Starr (later of a Rick Rubin-created "supergroup" The Four Hosemen). SIN recorded a demo produced by Dana Strum (Vinnie Vincent Invasion, Slaughter), and through Strum, Fox got introduced to Vinnie Vincent, who allegedly ripped off a few of Fox's songs.

Fox was interviewed in Penelope Spheeris' rock film *The Decline of Western Civilization Part II: The Metal Years*. That movie was successful, and with the exposure the future looked bright. He got a gig with Burn, a hard-hitting band of West Coast scenesters managed by Wendy Dio, Ronnie James Dio's wife. Needless to say, that didn't work out. Then he joined hard-working Arizona metal assassins Surgical Steel, who once backed Judas Priest's Rob Halford. But clashing egos assured that group's failure.

Fox had been in enough bands to know that his career was flatlining, so in a drastic departure from the rock business, he joined the California State Military Reserve. To further distance himself from his metal aspirations, he got deep into the Renaissance Fair scene. He then served four years as VP of the LA chapter of the Polish-American Congress. "Suligowski's Regiment of the Polish Commonwealth" works to raise Polish ethnic awareness. He claims to be from a noble bloodline going back to 1148. To further distance himself from rock, he became a CERT (Community Emergency Response Team) member.

Fox drifted a long way from the Sunset Strip, but he never gave up his bad-boy metal roots. He eventually returned to performing and recording, providing bass tracks to the Spiders and Snakes album *The Year of the Snake*. They covered the Angel version of The Young Rascals' "I Ain't Gonna Eat Out My Heart Anymore" (penned by Gloria Jones' collaborator Pam Sawyer). He played a Steeler reunion in 2013 at The Whisky A Go Go. Fox also devotes time to rock charity functions and all-star jams.

As a sideman he bounced from band to band in the second tier of hair metal. W.A.S.P. and Steeler were pivotal acts but were light years from the fame and glory of Motley Crüe or GNR. He experienced the frustration of the mid-level band that runs into a brick wall. They do everything right: the music is competent, but fame never materializes. You can have all the right hair and clothes and guitars and chops, but in metal, many are called and few are chosen.

Fox has to fight for any shred of recognition. Some people seem to have a problem with him, some for taking credit for the rise of W.A.S.P., while others condemn his Polish heritage promotion as supporting White Power. Such hot-button topics have resulted in his being tossed off Facebook more than once.

He was a product of the hair metal revolution. When that music was in its heyday, his future

Rik Fox, hair metal hero, Surgical Steel, 1986. Photo by Michael Richard Sneeburger. Courtesy of the Rik Fox Archives.

looked bright. When the epoch ended, his dreams ended with it. He had no chance of making it in the Nirvana generation.

Rik Fox: "I've been lucky to have been around all these scenes: glitter rock in the 70s in New York, Sunset Strip metal in the 80s, and all the stuff that has come since. The 80s was a great time in LA, and I have my place in it all. Steeler and W.A.S.P. and SIN all played huge parts in musical history. Rock and roll remains a major part of my life, and I plan to still keep doing this until they stick me in my grave." ●

CHARLIE FARREN

LR010

People know that when I walk in the room I am a rock 'n' roller

— JOE PERRY PROJECT, "LISTEN TO THE ROCK"

CHARLIE FARREN was born to rock August 27, 1953. He was raised in the blue-collar towns of Everett and Malden, Massachusetts, and played guitar in 70s Boston-area rock cover bands. His first group doing original material, Balloon, blew up on the local scene in 1980 with a fiery demo hot on FM stations across New England.

Atlantic Records loved the demo and signed the group. But then Ahmet Ertegun recruited Farren to replace Ralph Moreman as the vocalist of Aerosmith guitarist Joe Perry's solo band, Joe Perry Project. As a Boston rocker, Farren jumped at the chance to play with his hero.

He toured and recorded the second Joe Perry Project album, 1981's *I've Got the Rock'n'Rolls Again*, which featured a few Balloon tunes ("East Coast, West Coast," "Listen to the Rock") as well as Farren-Perry compositions. Highlights of that era included a US tour with Ozzy Osbourne and Def Leppard, and dates on Rush's *Moving Pictures* tour.

Despite the band's success, Farren felt it was time to move on. Joe Perry was in a bad way with drugs, and the band became a cesspool of second-stringers serving Joe's habit. Plus there was the omnipresent spectre of Steven Tyler, as well as the incessant chatter about an inevitable

Aerosmith reunion. And it was an uncomfortable gig, being the lead singer of a mid-level band named for a guitarist.

Farren's next band, The Enemy, enjoyed Northeast FM rock fame for their melodic metal, heard in 1985 on a single ("America Rocks"), local radio compilation ("Sally's Got a Poker Face"), and club dates opening for Twisted Sister, Blue Öyster Cult, and his former boss' band Aerosmith. But The Enemy (with ex-Balloon members) fell apart over the usual mix of market rejection and bruised egos. Farren got some session work, such as guitar on Bad Company's *Fame and Fortune* and Nona Hendryx's *The Heat*. He'd seemingly developed enough cache to take his career to the next level.

In 1986, he formed a power trio, with Joe Perry Project/Ted Nugent bassist David Hull (Heit) and drummer John "Muz" Muzzy, that Foghat manager Tony Outeda signed to Warner Bros under the name(s) Farren/Heit or Farrenheit. 1987's *Farrenheit*, produced by Keith Olsen and promoted by a 75-date tour opening for hometown legends Boston, spent 17 weeks on the charts. But the album—an underrated effort, like an R&B Van Halen—got lost in hair metal's Aqua-Net haze. Warner never put out their second album, due to legal issues with their name. For Farren, failure was becoming the norm.

Charlie Farren is still rockin', Boston, 2014. Photo by Paul Lydon. Courtesy of Charlie Farren.

Farren had band after band after band, each of them ever so close, on the cusp of fame, and yet nothing happened. Each time there were high hopes, backed by big-time production and promotional budgets. He was a bonafide rock star around Fenway, forever linked to the Aerosmith family, with an amazing resume of major-label records and tours, and could drink for free across the chowder-head region. Yet he was blue-collar enough to know that such cache was never gonna put food on the table for his growing family.

Farren gave up his rock star dreams in the 90s to support his wife and three daughters, working day jobs at Compaq and Hewlett-Packard. He continues to make solo records around his 9-to-5, able to turn his music career into an adult hobby.

His half-dozen 21st-century recordings include work with local luminaries like Peter Wolf (J. Geils Band), Jon Butcher (Jon Butcher Axis), and Joey McIntyre (New Kids on the Block). The title track to Farren's 2007 *Tuesday* was a tune composed by Boston singer Brad Delp, whose suicide deeply shook Farren.

Charlie Farren should be a household name. But he seems resigned to his fate, and is not into sour grapes: "I'm completely self-absorbed. People ask me what I like to listen to. I say I don't listen to anything. I listen to my stuff. I put on my headphones and work on my music. They ask me what I do for fun. I tell 'em that *is* what I do for fun. What I do for fun isn't put on other people's music. I was never into that." ●

LROII

GLORIA JONES

I'll be your shelter in the time of storm
All you gotta do is call

— GLORIA JONES, "SHARE MY LOVE"

GLORIA JONES is a beautiful and talented musician whose story spans from the African-American churches of Cincinnati and Los Angeles, to the hippest London clubs, to the heartland of West Africa. She navigated disparate music scenes, from Sunday morning gospel, to Sunset Strip rock and roll, to Motown funk and soul, to underground glam and punk rock. And her interracial, taboo love affair with the late Marc Bolan generated plenty of problems. Today, Gloria should have a chip on her shoulder. Instead she dropped out of the limelight to become a mother and humanitarian activist.

Gloria Richetta Jones was born October 19, 1948 in Cincinnati, Ohio. She grew up in the Pentecostal church, singing in the choir of her parents, minister Richard "Baby" Jones and his wife, pianist LaVerne Jones.

"I was very blessed. At two years old, my uncle was my babysitter. He was a postman and an aspiring jazz musician in Cincinnati, and he practiced at my father's church. I'd sit there as he rehearsed and I'd pretend that was my piano. I was very emotional when he played. So that was the beginning of Gloria Jones."

Her father recognized her musical talents, as well as those of his son Richard. He saw stardom in her future. He relocated his family to LA when Gloria was just seven years old so the kids could grow up around the music industry. Over time, "Elder Jones," as her dad was known, evolved into a prominent preacher. He was handsome and could preach and sing, and the ladies loved him. According to Gloria, he became known as "the Frank Sinatra of The Church of God in Christ."

"I performed my first solo at the age of four," Gloria recalls. "My mom thought it was a little child getting up to sing 'Yes Jesus Loves Me.' But they said I got up there and belted out 'When I Lost My Baby I Almost Lost My Mind.' The church was not only shocked that I had performed that song, but also by my interpretation of the song."

Gloria Jones, family photo with mother LaVerne, father Richard, and brother Richard. Cincinnati, OH circa 1952. Collection of Gloria Jones.

all students at San Fernando High School, also included Gloria's cousin Billy Preston (later known as "the fifth Beatle"), gospel legend Andrae Crouch, Frankie Kahrl (who did 1968's "Don't Be Afraid Do As I Say"), Edna Wright (of Honey Cone, and sister of Darlene Love) and future soul star Sondra "Blinky" Williams. The Cogics album spawned two 1964 singles, sold mostly at local gospel shows: "It Will Never Lose Its Power" was composed by Crouch (and became the basis of his future hit "The Blood Will Never Lose Its Power"), and "It's a Blessing."

"We were on Vee Jay at the same time as The Beatles, and we knew that things started shifting because we were working with Richard Simpson. This was when the race records were first coming up. You had Chess Records, but then you had Motown with a new generation of hits. The Cogic Singers were pushed as 'the teenage wonders' and we'd win all the gospel awards. But we were never going to make money."

"My dad said to me, 'Even though I'm a minister, I want you to make something of your career.' So he gave me permission to go into show biz when I was 17. That was a real embarrassment to the family because the church said I left God. So my parents were ridiculed and lost respect. But my dad really felt that I could make something of myself.

"My father went with me on all of my interviews. The industry respected that he was a minister. My father asked one thing of the management company. I had just turned 18 and he asked that I would not be abused or used sexually in the industry, which made it difficult sometimes because when I went on the road with the promoters, after a TV show, they'd take me straight to my room. I'd say, 'Can't I have a milkshake?' and they were like, 'No, we're not allowed to talk to you or look at you. We have to take you straight to your room.' But I had a clean spirit."

Mother LaVerne worked two jobs so Gloria could study classical piano. As a teenager she practiced Mozart during the week, and then belted out gritty gospel for her dad's Sunday services. "Those two weren't mixing at all," Gloria recalls. "So I had to find a balance. I competed in the national awards for classical musicians. I was playing some Bach and I got so into it, I went off into some gospel. The judges got upset, but this one lady judge said, 'Leave her alone and let her create.' So I feel that I've always been given a chance."

By age 14, Gloria was starring in a well-known gospel group assembled by her father. The Cogics, or The Cogic Singers (The Church of God in Christ Singers), made secular inroads with 1963's *It's a Blessing* LP for producer Richard "Bishop" Simpson's gospel label Simpson Records, distributed by Vee Jay. The group of preachers' children,

LA's gospel and soul scenes intertwined. Cogics fan and Motown executive Hal Davis introduced Gloria to Ed Cobb, a white pop star with eight gold records as a member of The Four Preps. Cobb managed The Standells and wrote their hit "Dirty Water."

"The industry heard about The Cogics and came to find us. There was Sam Cooke's manager J.W. Alexander, and then Frank Wilson who was the big producer at Motown at the time, and Hal Davis, another Motown producer. The next thing I knew I got work doing a background vocal session with Brenda and Patrice Holloway. Hal Davis looks at me and says, 'I've got something for you.' The next day I go meet Ed Cobb, who'd just written Brenda's 'Every Little Bit Hurts.' Hal says, 'Ed has this great song I want you to try.' It was 'Heartbeat.'"

Ed Cobb's Greengrass Productions was the force behind Gloria's March 1965 R&B cut "Heartbeat (Parts 1 & 2)" for Uptown Records. The song later grazed the charts as recorded by both Dusty Springfield and Spencer Davis Group. Gloria's cousin Billy Preston recorded the same song as an instrumental. The single did well locally but never became a hit.

"Everybody was excited about 'Heartbeat.' I thought it was coming out on Motown but it came out on Uptown. These are the experiences and the moments of being naive. And I feel that is the reason, after 40-plus years, I can still laugh about it all. I was blessed to have Berry Gordy recognize my talents. I remember Brenda said to him, 'Mister Gordy, this is my friend Gloria Jones, the singer of 'Heartbeat.' He said, 'No, she is Gloria Jones, the songwriter.'"

Gloria Jones (far right), The Cogics (Church of God in Christ Singers), 1963, with Billy Preston, Andraé Crouch, Edna Wright, and Blinky Williams. Collection of Gloria Jones.

The love we share Seems to go nowhere

— **GLORIA JONES, "TAINTED LOVE"**

GLORIA JONES' ORIGINAL VERSION of "Tainted Love" came out in May 1965 on Champion Records. The song, composed by Cobb, was the B-side to "My Bad Boy's Comin' Home" but it garnered more attention than the intended hit. Similar to "Heartbeat," the record failed to tear up the charts. In 1981, it got reworked into a million-seller by the electro/new wave act Soft Cell.

"I'm gonna tell you the truth. I never liked 'Tainted Love.' But when an artist doesn't like a song, that's always the hit! I don't know if it was because I was a minister's daughter and maybe 'tainted' was sinful… But when Soft Cell had the hit, I was thrilled for them."

1966's 11-song album *Come Go With Me* (Uptown), produced by Cobb and arranged by his Hollywood High classmate Lincoln Mayorga, featured her next two singles: The Supremes-like "Finders Keepers" b/w "Run One Flight of Stairs," and the doo-wop-style "Come Go with Me" b/w "How Do You Tell an Angel" (the latter A-side a cover of The Del-Vikings' 1957 hit). The front-cover, full-color shot showed the young lovely in a miniskirt and go-go boots. The back cover jacket exalted, "The New 'Heartbeat' Sound that Never Quits," while liner notes extolled, "It won't be long before Jones-style excitement is the sure-fire criterion by which all hit sounds and hit makers are judged."

Even though Gloria performed on TV and got played on the radio, she was not The Supremes or Gladys Knight. Fame would keep eluding her. In baseball parlance, there were lots of singles and doubles but no home runs.

L: Gloria Jones, *Come Go With Me*, Uptown Records, 1966. Photo by George Jerman. Courtesy of Gloria Jones.

Opposite: Los Angeles post-performance shots: with Jerry Lee Lewis in *Catch My Soul*, 1968, and with *Shindig* host Jimmy O'Neill, December 1965. Collection of Gloria Jones.

Climb the walls and eat your heart but it ain't gonna do you no good You double-crossed me now you lost me because you didn't treat me like you should

— GLORIA JONES, "FINDERS KEEPERS"

GLORIA'S POPULARITY LED to appearances on mid-6os teen dance TV shows like *Shindig* (two episodes in December 1965), *Hollywood A Go-Go* (New Year's Day 1966) and *The Regis Philbin Show* (Philbin's first TV show, on KOGO in San Diego, in early 1965).

Jones' music career was taking off, and at the same time she attended Cal State LA, where she studied classical piano and befriended tennis-player Billie Jean King. Gloria's arts department connections led to roles in independent stage productions like 1968's *Catch My Soul* (Jack Good's

rock rendition of *Othello* with Jerry Lee Lewis and Dr. John) and *Revolution* (at the newly-built Mark Taper Forum, intended to be the West Coast's answer to Lincoln Center).

In 1969, she starred in the original LA cast of *Hair*, funded by The Smothers Brothers. Many cast members were future stars: Jennifer Warnes, Melba Moore, Meatloaf, and glam-rocker Jobriath. After one show, Jobriath brought a few *Hair* actors to a soiree thrown by Miss Mercy of the Frank Zappa-linked group The GTO's. The event was a party for the British band Tyrannosaurus

Rex. There, Jobriath introduced Gloria to T. Rex's frontman Marc Bolan.

"Jobriath was ahead of his time and was misunderstood, but he was a true artist. He was an intellectual. He had no limits, coming out a time when the psychedelic era became clean again with bands like Three Dog Night. So Jobriath had a new energy and people did not want it or accept it. They condemned it. He to used to always come sit with us in the dressing room. He said that there was a party for Tyrannosaurus Rex, and convinced me to go with him. Marc came in with his beautiful satin sleeves and his velvet pants and platform heels like 'I'm here!' And I was on the piano like 'I'm here!' And there weren't going to be two stars. So he just sashayed past me and walked off.

"But to make a long story short, there was a connection. Then I didn't see him for another two years, but each time there was always a stronger connection. Later on I asked him, 'Did you know about me when I was singer in 1965?' and he said, 'No, I didn't know anything about you.' But Marc was a mod, and the mods were the children who represented 'Tainted Love.' But he'd never admit it."

During this time, she met British-born lyricist Pam Sawyer. The two became Motown's first female songwriter/producer team, behind almost-smashes for The Jackson 5 ("2-4-6-8," "Christmas Won't Be the Same this Year"), The Four Tops ("Just Seven Numbers [Can Straighten Out Your Life]"), Marvin Gaye ("My Mistake [Was To Love You]"), Gladys Knight & The Pips ("If I Were Your Woman"), Jr. Walker ("Take Me Girl, I'm Ready"), and The Supremes ("Have I Lost You"). In the Motown system, one couldn't be both a singer and a writer so the tunes written by Pam and Gloria got credited to "LaVerne Ware," her mother's birth name.

"I met Pam Sawyer at Motown Records in 1968. I was waiting for Hal Davis. He was the kind of producer you'd wait for hours to see because you knew that he'd give you a chance. I was playing chords in the music room and Pam knocked on the door and said, 'I like your feel.' She asked, 'Do you write?' And I said, 'A few songs, but I'm not really a professional writer.' She came over to my place one night because I had a piano, and every song we wrote was just incredible… 'If I Were Your Woman' we wrote in 30 minutes. 'Just Seven Numbers' I once heard in an elevator in Switzerland…"

Motown was a competitive world. Gloria and Pam were talented but they never fit in. "We were female producers, but we were real women. Pam wore full-length sable furs and a giant rock. She just wanted to write. I just wanted to write and produce. But the males said, 'How can this be? There's no room for female writers.' So now you had two girls saying, 'How do we crack this?'"

Their first session, at Motown Studios in Detroit was with The Funk Brothers and Dennis Coffey. "I said, 'Pam, we're gonna go in there and wear hot pants. We have to break the sexual barrier…' We wore those hot pants in there; we had long Charo-type hair and Pam was in her long sable furs. Those musicians said, 'Who are these ladies?' We said, 'We're songwriters and producers. What would you like to drink?' Big mistake! We got them so toasted, they had to come back the next day and record for us. But we had to break the ice."

The newest Motown duo worked with the early Commodores as producers of the group's first hit, "The Zoo (The Human Zoo)." Jones and Sawyer recognized the star qualities of Lionel Richie as more than just another accompanying musician after he sang on a few of Gloria's studio "scratch demos" (reference tracks).

and said, 'We can't hear it with this guy Walter Orange.' She asked what we thought and we said, 'Why not the sax player?' He wasn't the best sax player. But we were the first producers to put Lionel behind the microphone. James Carmichael was our arranger at first. So The Commodores grew, but their base never drifted far from what Pam and I first gave them."

Gloria sang background vocals on legendary rock records, though not always credited. Her contributions can be heard on Ike & Tina Turner's "Proud Mary," Little Feat's "Dixie Chicken," Jackie DeShannon's "Put a Little Love in Your Heart," Lynyrd Skynyrd's "Sweet Home Alabama," *Phil Spector's Christmas Album*, the *Neil Young* album, Rolling Stones' *Beggars Banquet*, and Steve Harley's *Hobo With A Grin*.

"Brenda Holloway, Patrice Holloway, and I had a great sound that was needed in the industry. REO Speedwagon, Elvin Bishop, Ry Cooder, Van Dyke Parks—we worked with Bonnie Bramlett. We were bringin' that gospel sound to California. But we were innocent. We did a session for Barry White when he was 19 and he had no money. He was good friends with Brenda, who said, 'Barry, don't worry, just buy us a hamburger.' So we were doing innocent business, but not realizing we were making business. We didn't have anything; we were just going with our feelings. Sometimes we recorded ten sessions in one day. We were young and doing it for cash.

Gloria Jones, Los Angeles, 1973. Photo by Jim Britt. Courtesy of Gloria Jones.

"Suzanne de Passe [Motown exec] asked if we'd take The Commodores into the studio. And Pamela has an excellent ear. We took the band in the studio and Walter Orange, the drummer, was the lead singer. Pamela was running around crazy, going, 'He's too James Brown! We want to go pop! We want to cross over!' She always said, 'You make money when you cross over.' Lionel Richie doesn't remember but we called Suzanne

"In 1973 I was in Europe with Joe Cocker. We performed at Crystal Palace with The Beach Boys, and Marc was coming out of The Speakeasy. Joe was taking us out for dinner for our last night in England. Marc saw Joe and said, 'Hey Joe, you better be careful, don't let those girls rob you.' Joe said, 'Oh no man, these are my stage singers, they're going back to the States tomorrow.' We all just laughed!"

Gloria Jones, with Marc Bolan, T. Rex drummer David Lutton, and fans, Newark Theater, Nottingham, England, February 1976. Photo courtesy of Fee Warner/TAG (T. Rex Action Group).

Shining on the outside get the impression Thinking on the inside lost expression

— GLORIA JONES, "TIN CAN PEOPLE"

GLORIA AND MARC drifted back together when she got hired to sing background vocals for a T. Rex concert at San Francisco's Winterland Theater in October 1972. The two became inseparable— though both were legally married to others.

The lovebirds contributed to the Ike & Tina classic "Nutbush City Limits," recorded in May 1973 at Ike's Bolic Sound Studios in Inglewood, California. "I was one of the Ikettes on 'Proud Mary,' 'Higher,' and 'Nutbush City Limits.' Mr. Ike Turner loved our sound with Tina, so he'd call at three or four o'clock in the morning. It didn't matter; we'd go meet him and Tina in the studio and record. I always kept a respectful relationship with Ike and Tina.

"So when Marc and I came into town, I called Ike and I told him that I was with my boyfriend, and he invited us to the studio. He said, 'Bring him down. Tell him to bring his guitar.' Tina was there singing 'Nutbush City Limits' and he asked me to put down the background voices. Ike had Marc sit next to him in the studio. Then the two went out and discussed guitar parts. Marc came in and started cranking up his guitar and he began playing, and he turned the song into a whole 'nother groove. That guitar sound is nobody but Marc Bolan. Through me, Marc also played with Ray Parker, Jr., Eddie Green, Lonnie Jordan, Ollie Brown, Scott Edwards, and Sylvester Rivers; that was Marc's T. Rex band in America. He wanted to take that energy to England."

You came into my life from a brand new world
When your lips touched mine I became a slave to your world

— GLORIA JONES, "SO TIRED (OF THE WAY YOU'RE TREATING OUR LOVE BABY)"

WITH ALL HER session work and live perfor-mances, Gloria had less time to compose for others. But she found time to focus on her solo album. 1973's *Share My Love* (Motown) offered a mix of funk, soul, and disco—like a female Barry White with lush orchestrations.

The Tom Thacker-produced, Paul Riser-arranged opus included an Afrocentric cover shot of Gloria with a big fro and dashiki straight out of *Shaft* or *Cleopatra Jones*. Funky songs like "So Tired (Of the Way You're Treating Our Love Baby)," "Baby Don'tcha Know (I'm Bleeding for You)," and the title track, employed incredible musicians of various nationalities: African-American, Native American, Japanese, Jamaican, and Brazilian. "It wasn't a record about race; it was about musical expression and personal freedom." The complex lyrics and tortured themes embodied the heart-ache and struggle of her budding transcontinen-tal romance with the flamboyant British-Jewish rock legend Bolan.

"During that time touring, I'd decided I was going to make an innovative soul album not using Motown artists, but talented live musicians making soul music. Stevie [Wonder] and all them were going into technical aspects of recordings. We wanted the musicians to come into the studio and just play.

"The business was tough and I had to think about survival. I was in a situation where jealousy came in and I wasn't being called to sing background sessions. Brenda got into gospel, Patrice did her own thing, so nobody was calling me. I felt these people were taking food out of my mouth. That's one reason I decided to do an album. But the musical urge was coming on strong."

Gloria transitioned into her new role as a Motown artist. Upon completing *Share My Love* she got assigned powerful management and a full-fledged publicity campaign that included four-color ads and a Sunset Strip billboard. Everybody involved in the project anticipated big things.

"When I started putting the album together," she recalls, "it started sounding pretty good. It was a time when women were a bit riskier, and it was a time of change. So when I made *Share My Love*, Motown said, 'We're gonna push you.' The management said, 'We're gonna push you.' There was an incredible producer. Everyone was ready."

Top: Gloria Jones, Los Angeles, 1972. Photo by Jim Britt.

Bottom: *Share My Love*, Motown, 1973. Photo by Fred Marx. Collection of Tony Mann.

Opposite: Gloria London, 1973. Photo by Keith Morris. Courtesy of Gloria Jones.

Getting high, running wild among all the stars above Sometimes it's hard to believe you remember me

— **GLORIA JONES**, "HIGH"

GLORIA SHOCKED HER management in November 1973 with a bombshell, announcing that she was in love with Marc Bolan and abandoning her solo career to join him in London. It was so crazy that no one reacted angrily. But for that offense, Motown banished her from the kingdom and shelved the LP. (It finally saw the light of day 36 years later.)

"Marc and I had just returned to LA from the Bahamas, and we took our limo to go see my billboard on the Sunset Strip. We got up there and he said, 'Well, your teeth look like camel's teeth.' He told the driver, 'Drive on…' I told Marc they really wanted to push this album, and he said, 'I'm going back to England, I'll call you and you let me know your decision…' So I get a call one night from Marc and he said, 'I was at a record shop and saw your album.' I said, 'Why are you worrying me about this?' The next week he called again and said, 'Well, I've decided. We can't live without each other so you've got to move to England.' So I called the management, called the record company, called the production company, and said, 'I'm in love…' and I got on a plane."

Gloria remembers Motown's reaction: "Well, let's just say they forgave me and I forgave them; we all forgave each other. The management was puzzled because they were successful people and they didn't understand it. Sometimes I think I could've worked that out, but it was Marc's time to tour, and he really needed me."

I grew all debonair When I had the 1980s air, in your hair

— MARC BOLAN & GLORIA JONES, "CITY PORT"

IN LONDON, GLORIA INJECTED spirit and substance into the East Ender's glam-rock band, T. Rex. She played clavinet and sang on five T. Rex LPs: 1974's *Light of Love* and *Zinc Alloy and the Hidden Riders of Tomorrow*, 1975's *Bolan's Zip Gun*, 1976's *Futuristic Dragon*, and 1977's *Dandy in the Underworld*. Critics still don't know what to make of that punk-gospel fusion, but Gloria imposed her soulful style on the U.K. hard rock scene.

"We were musicians and Marc was ready for change, the world was ready for change, but no one wanted change. The world had just come out of psychedelia, and then we lost Jimi Hendrix, we lost Janis, so it all came back as Sly Stone, which was a huge change. Neil Bogart at Casablanca Records loved change, and he gave Marc the money for the *Light of Love* album. And look how big KISS became. But people couldn't accept the fact that disco had come in. They didn't understand it and they tried to get rid of it."

Jones bristles at the idea that some T. Rex fans saw her like a Yoko Ono-type interloper. Fans did confront them in airports and eateries, but the star couple never took the bait. They traveled in jet-set circles from London to Monaco to LA. But it was still a segregated world, so the flamboyant interracial lovers caused sociological consternation.

"We were pushing so many boundaries," Gloria explains. "We had new sounds, with hi-hats and clavinets. Marc was doing different things with his guitar sound. I mean we were going heavy. We

were going for change—innovative and futuristic ideas that are just now happening. He wanted to change, but the fans did not want him to change. They never accused me of changing anything. They saw he was happier with the direction that he was going in. He was a creator who wanted to move into making films. In 1972/73 he was already recording videos in Paris."

Gloria became pregnant but continued playing in the band for several more months. On September 26, 1975, she gave birth to Rolan Bolan (Rolan Seymour Feld). "I believe that Marc knew everything he wanted to do in life. He never thought he'd have the chance to be a family man, but he took that time out to be a family man with Rolan and myself. He was a kind person and a misunderstood person. He was genuine, but he was in an industry where people didn't accept honesty and individuality. The industry attitude was, 'I can kill your dog but you can't kill my cat.'"

Come rain, come shine, you're always on my mind
Come loving, come hate, my heart's anticipating

— GLORIA JONES, "WINDSTORM"

A HAPPY MOM, Gloria got back to her own music with 1976's *Vixen*. The U.K.-only album, produced by she and Marc for T. Rex's label EMI, included a funky breakdown of "Bang i Gong (Get It On)," her ballad "Go Now" about leaving it all behind for love, and an updated "Tainted Love." Weeks later, the couple cut a single as Marc Bolan & Gloria Jones, retooling Phil Spector on "To Know You Is To Love You."

In early 1977, Gloria honed her studio skills arranging and producing (with her brother Richard Jones) the 13-piece British disco group Gonzalez. Their hit "Haven't Stopped Dancin' Yet" resulted in her joining the act on high-profile tours opening for Osibisa and Bob Marley & the Wailers. EMI promoted those dates with a Gloria Jones/Gonzales split single. Gloria's A-side "Bring on the Love" was hyped for its length of 7:14 ("714" a nickname for Quaaludes). Gonzalez's Gloria-produced flipside "Carnival" remains one of the era's great forgotten dancefloor jams. Gloria and Richard also produced the band's 1980 album *Watch Your Step*.

"Gonzalez was a serious jazz group. I mean, I had to lock the studio doors so that they couldn't leave because they did not want to record 'Haven't Stopped Dancin' Yet' and I knew it was a hit. I called Marc in a panic, telling him that I had a problem in the studio and he said, 'Well, I guess you'll just have to lock the doors.' I think he was just kidding but I told the engineer to lock the doors. But it was their real resentment towards disco... We were fortunate that Don Taylor gave Gonzalez a shot to open for Bob Marley on his first European tour. But Don said, 'You've got to let Gloria Jones sing with you.' What we did together was innovative."

While most established rockers mocked the emerging punk scene, Marc and Gloria were smack in the middle of it. Mark hired The Damned to open T. Rex's 1977 U.K. tour. He endorsed upstart groups like the Ramones, Generation X, Siouxsie & The Banshees, and Boomtown Rats. Bolan had such groups perform on his TV show, *Marc*.

"When we were at that [first London] Ramones show and they started doing the pogo, Marc was off to the front of the stage and I was panicked. But he was in his element. So Marc was really the godfather of punk. He and [Damned bassist] Captain Sensible really gelled because he found Captain to be a true intellectual; they were both voracious readers. He saw the change coming."

In the early hours of September 16, 1977, Gloria was driving Marc home in his electric-purple Mini Cooper GT. She missed a tight turn off an old horse bridge and collided with a large oak tree. The crash killed the 29-year-old Bolan. Marc, known for his love of cars but who never drove, died in the one-car wreck a mile or so from

THIS is the newest group on the pop scene: singers Marc Bolan and Gloria Jones, with their baby son Rolan Bolan.

The 6lb. 6oz. baby, born at a London clinic on Friday, made a quiet camera debut yesterday.

He should soon get used to the routine. His father, Marc One, will be back before the BBC-TV cameras next week — singing his latest song, Dreamy Lady.

The programme: Top of the Pops. The natural place, really, for a new father.

Picture: DOREEN SPOONER

Left: Gloria Jones with Marc Bolan and baby Rolan, London, September 1975. Photo credited to Doreen Spooner.

Right: Gloria onstage with T. Rex, Glasgow, 1976. Public domain.

his South-West London mansion after partying at a nightclub.

Gloria was taken to Queen Mary's Hospital with a shattered leg, busted jaw, facial injuries, severe internal injuries, and crushed vocal cords. She was hurt so badly, she only learned of Marc's death after his September 20 funeral. During her extended hospitalization, fans and scavengers pillaged their home for memorabilia, so Gloria lost all her personal effects and anything related to she and Marc.

Gloria accidentally killing her lover in a car wreck put a stop to everything. Her life and career were going great, and then both came to a crashing halt as a direct result of the accident. Gloria and Rolan endured decades of financial hardship in LA because she and Marc were never officially married. But Rolan benefited from the generosity of his godfathers. One godfather, David Bowie, who he never met, paid for his education from private school through college. Another godfather, Ringo Starr, directed 1997's *Born to Boogie* a concert film involving a 1972 T. Rex show.

Marc's death devastated Gloria. "You've got circumstances beyond your control. You're suddenly in a situation no one was expecting. So sometime in life it's better to just go on. It's just life, and my life at this time is for this legacy to live on because the music is alive."

My life is feeling much better now
I've wanted to hold you so long
I just want to show some affection now
I hope you can hear my song

— GLORIA JONES, "BRING ON THE LOVE"

1978'S *WINDSTORM* (Capitol), produced by her brother Richard, had been in the pipeline for some time. The eight-song LP featured smooth Gloria Gaynor-ish disco like "Bring on the Love," "Woman Is a Woman," and "Blue Light Microphone." The liner notes read: "Dedicated to the memory of my son's father, the late Marc Bolan, who we all miss very much."

In 1981, British electro-pop duo Soft Cell ressurected Jones' 1964 single "Tainted Love." The song shot to number one. That resulted in Gloria and writer Ed Cobb reconnecting. Ed co-wrote and co-produced 1982's *Reunited* for Ray Harris' MCA-distributed AVI imprint. The album, which spawned the risqué single "Body Heat" b/w "Sixty Minutes of Making Love" (also credited to Marc's memory), included a new reworking of "Tainted Love." Brian Chin wrote in *Billboard* (3/12/82): "Cobb's material is uneven but his production and Jones' singing are impressive, combining old soul, new funk, and the idiosyncratic, moody atmosphere that made Jones'

other albums so compelling." Such accolades yielded minimal chart impact.

Gloria went on with her life. Her involvement in the music industry waned over time. There were no more solo albums, but she still stayed active. She was next heard of at the dawn of the rap era.

Rolan Bolan: "My mom went through different phases but at the point after my father died, the main thing for her was to become a mother and raise my family and get through that step of her life. Once she got more at ease, she was able to reunite with her musical side and worked on projects. She was involved in the rise of LA hip hop, helping develop Ice T and Ice Cube. She always had vision. I thought everyone's parents were rock stars but I look back at it all in amazement. Other mothers were hosting Tupperware parties; we were at the studio until late at night. When I tell people my mother is *the* Gloria Jones, that often means more than Marc Bolan. It's exciting seeing her receive her due."

Marc Bolan & Gloria Jones singles, EMI UK, 1977:
"City Port" and "To Know You Is to Love You." Courtesy of Gloria Jones.

Evening News covers regarding the death of Marc Bolan, September 1977.
Collection of Tony Mann.

Beautiful dawn— melt with the stars again Do you remember the day when my journey began?

— GLORIA JONES, "HIGH"

IN 2010, GLORIA FOUNDED the Marc Bolan School for Music and Film in the "Blood Diamonds" killing fields of Makeni, Sierra Leone. Despite official corruption and myriad logistical hurdles, Gloria, an African-American mom from a different world, persevered. The odyssey began a decade earlier when Gloria travelled to West Africa to work with upcoming musicians. The poverty she saw motivated her to do something meaningful. Sierra Leone is a worst-case scenario: a chaotic, war and disease-ravaged nation.

"Rolan and I go there and embrace the children, some of who were former child soldiers. Marc loved the children, so his music lives on through these children. We're not looking to build the world's biggest school. We just want to help these young people to be able to have their own businesses composing music and editing film, so that they have a purpose for being. What better thing than to film yourself to discover who you are? Our projects are here to help. Marc was someone who helped. So we continue with our new and extended families. We are together as a family."

Gloria Jones, interviewed for *Lost Rockers*, author's apartment, New York, 2009. Photo by Tony Mann.

Good things still come Gloria's way. UNICEF rewarded her humanitarian efforts by having her sing with Swiss mixologist Pascal G on a benefit album. She appeared in the Oscar-winning film *20 Feet from Stardom*. She can now be heard on reissues of the long-forgotten 1969 album *Dylan Gospel*, by The Brothers and Sisters of LA, a group of black Angeleno vocalists who recorded gospel-flavored Bob Dylan songs with producer Lou Adler. In late 2014, Gloria was quarantined with the other villagers during the Ebola outbreak, but emerged from the ordeal in good health.

"She's an incredible lady," Rolan says. "She overcame so many tribulations and she always stayed strong. She's been such an inspiration. And now to pick a challenge even more intense in Africa is so amazing. To see her in action— and all these people embrace her and love her because she's lived up to her words. She's over there doing something beautiful: walking the land with the kids, eye-to-eye, hand-in-hand, and I give her so much love and respect for that. These kids in Africa can express themselves and realize they are not alone. And music is something that we all share.

"It can seem bizarre that the legacy of British glam rocker Marc Bolan now touches base in Sierra Leone, West Africa," he adds. "But that's the full circle my mother and I made, the direction we've taken to overcome the fact that we lost my father."

Marc Bolan died young, with many legal loose ends, so third parties took most of his money. But artist's financial problems were not unfamiliar to Gloria.

"My father wrote 'Precious Lord Take My Hand,'" Gloria recounts. "Tommy Dorsey played this song at the revivals, and followed my dad's melodies, but my father never got credit. If you look in the hymnals, it says his name in the credits, so he had a name in the revival circuit. Well, the same thing happens to me. I'm in the studio recording 'Tainted Love.' The original version by Ed Cobb was a typical 4/4, so I totally changed it to fit for me, to be more of a gospel, Gloria Jones-style song. So I'm repeating my father. Look at all of the great performers: from theater to musicals, it's always something. I just think if you choose to be a personality, these are things you have to deal with. To be a star you have to understand it and have no problem with what comes with it."

Rolan never profited from T. Rex royalties until he filed a $2 million suit. In late 2014 Bolan's catalog was sold for $15 million, so Rolan will finally benefit from that legacy.

Rolan: "With Gloria Jones there was no smoke and mirrors. It was just about getting in there and keeping the integrity of the music and going out there and giving 100 percent at all times, and really leading with your heart and soul. There were a lot of beautiful times but she wasn't doing it for the money. She was surrounded by so many talented people, really bringing out the best in everyone, working together and not being selfish. She always walked a straight line, was honest, and helped others along the way. She's a survivor and has many more goals to achieve. We can all learn from that."

Fame slipped out of Gloria's grasp, and she never overcame the pain of accidentally killing the love of her life. Her potential went unrealized; the accident changed her life and stopped her progress. Fame would elude her evermore.

"The life of an artist is a good life," Gloria concludes, "but powerful decisions have to be made if you believe in yourself and the size of your own ideas. When Pamela and I were writing those songs in the 60s and 70s, it was a risk. When Holland-Dozier-Holland and Smokey and Stevie wrote their songs, those were risks, because Mr. Gordy always said, 'Is someone gonna buy that record or is someone gonna buy a sandwich?' That's what we were dealing with. So how do you continue with all this and not give up? And how do you embrace the ups and the downs? You never know who's life you're gonna touch. We were able as artists to touch lives. People around the world, even now, say things like, 'You bring so much joy to me' or 'I've been following you for years.' I'm honored. It's all about going back to the love." ●

CHRIS DARROW

LR012

Listen here, I don't fear
I don't want to be your whipping boy

— CHRIS DARROW, "WHIPPING BOY"

CHRIS DARROW may be the most prolific rock musician you've never heard of. He's a multi-instrumentalist proficient on guitar, bass, violin, banjo, dobro, lap steel, and mandolin. Born and raised (and still residing) in Claremont, California, he first explored musical curiosities as a kid at Claremont Folk Music Center, run by Charles and Dot Chase, the grandparents of Ben Harper (who covered Chris' "Whipping Boy" on his debut CD).

Darrow and future notable David Lindley played in an early 60s bluegrass act, Dry City Scat Band, and then in the Beatlesque band The Floggs. In 1966, he and Lindley formed the longhaired psychedelic group Kaleidoscope (that Jimmy Page is alleged to have hailed as his favorite band of all time). Kaleidoscope briefly enjoyed some critical notoriety, and Darrow got his first taste of success. The band made two albums, 1967's *Side Trips* and 1968's *Beacon from Mars*, and shared stages with Jimi Hendrix, The Doors, and The Grateful Dead. They played a December 1967 residency at Steve Paul's The Scene in New York. Leonard Cohen saw one of those shows, and hired them to play on his masterwork *Songs of Leonard Cohen*. Then, for the usual reasons, Kaleidoscope broke up, leaving Darrow high and dry.

His dreams of solo stardom got waylaid when he took a gig with the popular Nitty Gritty Dirt Band.

They had a hit (a cover of Jerry Jeff Walker's "Mr. Bojangles") but despite all their recognition and sales, they never made the big time. After three disappointing albums, Darrow and Nitty founder Jeff Hanna departed to form The Corvettes. That band made singles for the Beach Boys-associated Dot Records, produced by The Monkees' Mike Nesmith. After failing to seize the limelight, The Corvettes got work as backup bands for Linda Ronstadt and LA guitarist John Stewart. When they finally got to record an album, guitarist Bernie Leadon left to join The Flying Burrito Brothers and then co-founded The Eagles. The other Corvettes joined Nesmith's ill-fated First National Band. Darrow, abandoned by his peers, was back to square one.

The Corvettes' brush with fame whetted Darrow's appetite for stardom. After years of near misses and standing in the shadows of rock icons, he'd expected a hit. The Corvettes were geared and primed for life in the fast lane. But that never happened. Then he had to deal with the fact that his bandmate Bernie went on to cofound one of the most famous rock groups in the world.

Darrow eked out a living as a sideman, playing the music of others and embodying "20 feet from stardom"—working with stars yet essentially anonymous. He played violin on James Taylor's

1970 *Sweet Baby James*, and added hillbilly strings to recordings by Hoyt Axton, Harry Chapin, and John Fahey. The role of a sideman can be tough, and can fuel much frustration. There's a rush of fame and stardom, but it's not actually for you.

Despite his relative anonymity, Darrow had built up an impressive resume as a session player. Fantasy Records took notice. He was thrilled, but little did he know what he was stepping into. That label was notorious for not paying artists and for destroying Credence Clearwater Revival. The shyster label Fantasy lived up to its name. Darrow finally got his chance to make a solo record, 1972's slice of Americana, *Artist Proof*. The album went nowhere in America but across the pond it gained some traction. He maneuvered out of his Fantasy contract and fled to England to follow up on that modicum of success, resulting in 1973's *Chris Darrow* and 1974's *Under My Own Disguise*, both released by United Artists. For all practical purposes, those records failed to excite consumers.

Darrow returned to America to lick his wounds. He tried to get gigs but nothing materialized. All his old friends were too famous or too fucked up to return his calls. So he drifted in limbo for a few years, wondering what went wrong. He had made great records, worked with stars, and changed with the times, yet things never clicked. He no longer dreamed of stardom but rather of subsistence. Nonetheless, instead of surrendering he persevered, taking work where he could get it, and continuing to play publicly on a roots level for the love of his craft.

Like other 60s/70s characters, Darrow tried to get in on LA's 80s punk/new wave scene. He produced 1987's *Snake Handler* by Chris D of The Flesheaters, and played guitar for Angie Bowie, a gig arranged by his friend Kim Fowley. Darrow was responsible for some good musical moments,

but overall it just didn't work. His chops didn't jibe with the vibe.

Lost rockers status must run in the family because Chris' son Steven Darrow has had a similar long, strange trip. He played in the cult LA punk band The Decadents, then in Eva O's goth-rock pioneers Super Heroines, then in the punk/metal act Hollywood Rose (who mutated into Guns N' Roses after his departure), and Angel Rot with White Zombie guitarist Tom Five. Despite this work, he remains obscure.

Chris Darrow: "I started out playing music early in life and was performing in folk and bluegrass bands around LA when I was in my late teens. I played rock and roll, world beat, jug band, and country rock, and have kept moving on down the line searching for music that fits my moods. For almost 50 years I have continued down that road hoping to improve my writing and playing abilities. It will only end when I die." ●

Chris Darrow in the studio for *Artist Proof*, Fantasy Records, 1971. Photo by Steve Cahill. Courtesy of the Chris Darrow Archives.

GASS WILD & JOHNNY HODGE

Don't let nobody tell you
They're only tryin' to sell you

— LIGHTNING RAIDERS, "VIEWS"

GASS WILD AND JOHNNY HODGE have extensive rock pedigrees having played in a variety of 70s British bands. They came together for a while in Lightning Raiders, an almost-famous outfit lost to obscurity. Their sound and style and stories inspired the likes of Sex Pistols and Motörhead. Vexed by changing lineups, changing times, changing labels, and some very bad luck, Lightning Raiders recorded two albums but released just two UK-only singles.

The two aspiring rockers, whose paths intertwined over the years, seemed to have it all: connections, looks, chops. Yet they never hit that home run. In fact, their burnout was spectacular. Their fruitless mutual association amplified their individual failures, and illustrated how two wrongs don't make a right.

Gass Wild (Thomas Edwards) came from the West Midlands parish of Hereford.

"I loved music," Gass begins. "I used to dream about it. My brother is 13 years older than me,

so when I was three or four, I was hearing his Elvis Presley 78s and loving it all. I was hooked on rock and roll from the start. Growing up in the 60s shaped my life.

"When I was 13 in 1965, I was at boarding school and the house band played on the last day of school. I found myself fascinated by drums. A month later, I saw that same drum set in a music store for cheap and I got my mother to buy it. That's how I started. I taught myself playing along to records. I practiced in the top room of my house. I'd go outside the door and pretend I was backstage, and then walk into my bedroom and put the record on, and get behind the kit and start playing along. That was my first taste, imagining that I was onstage. Before that, I'd stand in front of a full-length mirror with a tennis racket, strumming it like a guitar.

"As I got older, I'd go to gigs to watch the drummer and go and talk to them afterwards and ask if I could have a go at the kit. That's how I met

Aynsley Dunbar—he was a cool guy. He thought I had the makings of a good drummer and encouraged me. I saw him play a few times. When I was 16, I played at a youth club and then at a school dance. My first proper show was a few years later at Hereford Racecourse opening for him [May 16, 1968]. It was Traffic, Aynsley Dunbar Retaliation, Elmer Gantry's Velvet Opera, and we were called The Stone Blues Band. It was a great start."

Johnny Hodge came from the tranquil countryside of Yeovil, Somerset but he did not have a tranquil life. "I came from a broken home," he explains. "I remember coming home from the mental hospital where my mother was incarcerated, and everything was awful. Seeing The Who play 'Anyway, Anyhow, Anywhere' on TV set me for life. I thought, 'That's the only sense I can see in this world.' Not to mention it was so well received. My parents split up, and I lived in this nice place in the beauty of Somerset. But I wanted more. There was a guitar around and a book about guitar playing. So I played that guitar obsessively. I was 12 years old, so it was 1965, an ideal time to be in England.

"When I was still at school I saw The Who two weeks after Woodstock and then I saw the Floyd," Hodge recalls. "It was halcyon days, man. The bands were incredible. I could never believe I was around such fantastic, magnificent, awesome music. The best group I ever saw was The Who on that particular occasion. I left home and went to Bath. It was all about drugs, man, psychedelics. I see myself as a psychedelic rock and roller, I do."

Gass Wild and Johnny Hodge met in 1971. On one occasion, they went to the site of the first Glastonbury Festival. Hodge stayed and helped build the famed pyramidal stage and helped put the show together. The two fell out of touch for years yet both stayed friendly with the famed British hippie-rock band Hawkwind, which spawned Lemmy, later of Motörhead.

"We met and spent this wonderful week in Hereford," Hodge recollects. "It was truly lawless! It was great. Then we went off to Glastonbury. And then we didn't see each other for almost nine years. I went to Glastonbury in 1971 and got on a work crew. The guy who was running it was this guy Thomas Crimble who'd just left Hawkwind. We got a group together called The Windfuckers that was like the house band for that first Glastonbury. To call your band that back then was commercial suicide. But I think that's precisely why Thomas chose that name. Basically that was my way out of a place that you didn't usually get out of. Gass and I come from very similar geographical places."

Gass Wild: "In 1971 I'd been living in Amsterdam. I came back to London, but was back in Hereford for the weekend and I ran into Peter Farndon, later of The Pretenders, who was also living in London. He gave me his address and told me look him up when I was back in town. I later stayed with Peter, and through him I met Lemmy. I also knew guys in Hawkwind before Lemmy joined them. I went along to the studio when they were mixing their second album. The next thing I knew, Lemmy joined Hawkwind. And then he got kicked out of Hawkwind and formed Motörhead. Later I had a band called Cyanide Sweeties and we were both recording in the same studio. One night we didn't have a bassist so Lemmy sat in. That was the start of Lemmy trying to get me gigs as a drummer because he liked how I played. We hit it off and became buddies. He inspired me a lot."

Johnny Hodge spent the mid-70s in Wales, where he teamed with a crew of aspiring rockers: "They were rich hippies. They had a lot of money and lived in Hampstead, and one of them was Elizabeth Taylor's son. We became this hippie band, gigging the Welsh countryside. Everyone in the band was buying farms in Wales and it was all quite groovy and stoned for a while. When that fell apart I moved to London."

I ain't addicted to cocaine,
I ain't addicted to hash
I got no habit for narcotics,
I don't need the cash

— LIGHTNING RAIDERS, "ADDICTION"

CYANIDE SWEETIES WAS a glitter-rock band with Rolling Stones connections. "In 1974, I played in Cyanide Sweeties with this guy who turned me on to the rock and roll dream," Gass remembers. "He sang and played guitar and wrote good songs. We were roommates and partners-in-crime. We'd sit around and talk and dream, get stoned and dream and dream. He had the Dolls/Brats glam sound and style of the day.

"We wanted to try to get on Rolling Stones Records, and through various drug dealers that supposedly sold them an ounce of this and an ounce of that, we found out that Keith Richards lived on Cheyne Walk in Chelsea, London on the banks of the Thames. One day we drove by and saw a silver-grey Ferrari Dino sitting by this beautiful townhouse with striped canopies on the windows. So I went and rang the bell and a voice came over the intercom. I said, 'Hello, I met Ronnie Wood at Olympic Studios and he said for Rolling Stones Records to speak to Mick or Keith.' And he said, 'Go hang about in the garden, I'll be down in a few minutes.' So I realized I was talking to Keith. I went back to the car and told my mate what happened, and we realized we didn't have a tape with us. So he rode off to get the tape. Keith obviously wanted to look in the garden and check me out.

"So a few minutes later the door opens and out comes Keith inviting me in. We walk in the kitchen and he says, 'Wanna cuppa tea?' The night before they were on *Top of the Pops* doing "It's Only Rock N Roll," so I told him that I dug the song. He said he thought it was a bit too raw to be a hit, and he was right, it only went to #11 on the charts. Then his henchman-bodyguard Spanish Tony arrived. Keith says, 'Wanna do some coke?' and pours out this huge mountain of blow. I thought he was gonna split it three ways but it was all for me, so up it went. Then he says, 'So what you doin?' and I explained that my partner was getting him our tape and a hit of morphine. He says, 'I've gotta go and do an interview, give them some show biz bullshit. We can tell them you're our new drummer.'

"So we get into his Ferrari and he sticks in an unmixed tape of the *It's Only Rock N Roll* album. So we drive off to the interview at the Stones' offices. Because I did all this coke, I started drinking loads of Jack Daniels. I must've gotten totally shitfaced because I woke up hours later with my head in a sink, and I get up and there must've been a glass shelf, and it shattered, and I had no idea where I was. Then I saw my singer and I realized I was back at Keith's. So I walked down a flight of stairs, and there's Anita Pallenberg sitting behind a desk, and it felt like a scene in *Performance*. She said, 'Keith's downstairs with your friend listening to music.' So I walk down and Keith's there and I apologize to him. He said, 'Aah, its cool, Jack Daniels is dynamite shit.'

I gave him some hash and we were all cool. I met him several times after that at his house; he'd lend us the Stones rehearsal gear. We'd go off and do these pub gigs with a truck filled with all this incredible gear. I'm sure as many people came to see the Stones gear as came to see us!"

Meanwhile, Johnny Hodge had developed into a hot guitarist. His druggy hippie friends brought him into a latter incarnation of The Pink Fairies, in which he became Johnny "Guitar" Hodge a.k.a. "Little John." He played on 1978's *Do It 77*, credited for legal reasons as Twink & The Fairies. Duncan "Sandy" Sanderson and Larry Wallis of the Fairies, as well as ill-fated T. Rex member Steve Peregrin Took, had played with Hodge as The Psychedelic Routers.

Johnny Hodge, London, 1977. Collection of Johnny Hodge.

Way back in '71 I spent a week in the sun, I suppose I was tryin' to prove it Rainbows under the sky, time stopped going by, and bands played psychedelic music

— LIGHTNING RAIDERS, "PSYCHEDELIC MUSIK"

LIGHTNING RAIDERS WAS BORN from the ashes of The Pink Fairies. Sandy Sanderson and Johnny Hodge formed Lightning Raiders (named for a 1945 Buster Crabbe film) with bassist Andy Allen, drummer Harry Lupino (nephew of actress Ida Lupino), and saxist Michael Wilding (son of Elizabeth Taylor). During that time, Hodge dated Michael's teenaged half-sister Liza Todd.

Hodge: "Joly McPhee said we were the Sex Pistols two years before the Pistols. We weren't a pub rock group; it was really raw and dangerous. Pub rock was big at the time, and it was very organized and neat and pristine. We weren't like that. Eddie and the Hot Rods and Dr. Feelgood and Brinsley Schwartz came out of that, too."

Lightning Raiders quickly earned a reputation as a solid act, drawing sizeable crowds at London rock clubs like Dingwall's and Camden Music Machine. The band's high-energy guitar mania made them part of the British Heavy Metal explosion that spawned Def Leppard, Iron Maiden, and Saxon. The Raiders shared stages with popular bands of the day, such as Motörhead, Girlschool, and The Stray Cats.

"We formed in 1977 and we had a residency at The Speakeasy," Hodge explains. "That was the famous London rock and roll hangout where you played four sets a night. Guys like Peter Townshend and Phil Lynott went there late-night to jam. Unlike other people that shall remain nameless, we didn't cut our hair—we maintained our style. The proper punks like the Pistols and Siouxsie used to come to our gigs after The Vortex because they respected the fact we hadn't run to the barber as soon as the rumble started."

Marc Bolan of T. Rex went to The Speakeasy late one night with writer BP Fallon, and Bolan jammed with Johnny Hodge, Andy Allen, Steve Jones of the Sex Pistols, and New York Dolls/Heartbreakers drummer Jerry Nolan. Bolan was so enthused, he planned to record with the Raiders a few weeks later. But Marc died in a car crash.

"BP Fallon turned up one night with Marc Bolan in 1977," Hodge recalls. "We played and he was impressed. It was incredible. Marc said, 'We'll go into the studio as soon as I finish my TV show.' I think this is where the bad luck started, because as soon as he finished that show he died in the car crash. In 1977 Elvis died, most of Thin Lizzy died, and my son was born three days after we played with Marc Bolan. So there was a hell of a lot going on that year. When I saw the headline that he died, I didn't know what to think. I was devastated by the loss of the most consummate

rock star I ever encountered. There was nothing disappointing about Marc Bolan himself. He was the real deal. He was an amazing fellow, charming—he looked great. For me, 1977 was a year of death and birth."

Andy Allen was friends with Steve Jones and Paul Cook of the Sex Pistols and played bass on the Pistols' "Silly Thing." Andy then brought in Jones and Cook to unofficially join Lightning Raiders. The lineup of Allen, Jones, Cook and Hodge played on March 1980's "Psychedelic Musik" b/w "Views" (Arista UK). That lineup, managed by Fallon, recorded a 45 that was co-produced by Jones at London's Wessex Studios. Soon after that, Allen, Jones and Cook quit the Raiders and formed The Professionals.

Hodge: "Lightning Raiders had psychedelic roots. We came out of Glastonbury but we weren't a hippie band. We weren't singing of peace and love. Our peers were The Pink Fairies and Hawkwind. We were very rock and roll and played well. Steve Jones and Paul Cook hung around with us a lot, soaking it in. Finally we did a record with them. In 1980, 'Psychedelic Musik' came out on Arista with Steve and me on guitar, Paul Cook on drums, and Andy on bass and vocals. Things were on the upswing. Then Andy left, so I was left high and dry. He quit, after we toured with Motörhead, to be in The Professionals. He never said that he was leaving, I read about it in the music press."

"When a new movement comes around, it tends to be quite fascistic," Hodge explains. "So people didn't understand how these Sex Pistols members would do a song called 'Psychedelic Musik.' It was supposed to be more like a Beach Boys song. How it turned into this punk song I don't know, but now you listen to it, it just sounds like a take on a Pistols track. It's like a Sex Pistols record with different lyrics. It didn't go anywhere."

The final Lightning Raiders single, "Criminal World," Island UK, 1981.
Collection of Tony Mann.

I'm gonna pose a serious threat
A credit to no one except for myself in this
criminal world

— LIGHTNING RAIDERS, "CRIMINAL WORLD"

GASS WILD SPENT most of the 70s partaking in cutting-edge sex, drugs, and rock and roll, splitting time between London, Paris, Brazil, and Hereford. Music circles led to Gass' drumming with New York Dolls/Heartbreakers guitarist Johnny Thunders as The Living Dead for a week in 1978 at Paris' Gibus Club.

Gass: "I wanted to audition for The Heartbreakers in 1977 after Jerry Nolan quit the band. But I read in *Sounds* he was looking for an American

replacement, so I never checked it out. Lemmy invited me to the *NME* Christmas party, so we go to this bash with The Flamin' Groovies and Dave Edmunds. I was sitting at a table watching a band and next to me is Johnny Thunders. I told him, 'I was gonna audition for you but I heard you wanted an American. You still looking for a drummer?' and he gave me his number.

"I'd go see him and he was doing dope then, and I have to admit that I dabbled, luckily only a little bit. In fact, one time he shot me up and said, 'Everyone who's ever played with me became a junkie.' I said, 'Well, I'm gonna be the exception, Johnny.' Seconds later, I was totally out of it. But thank God I've got clean arms. I never got deeply into it; otherwise we'd never be having this talk. But that's how I met Johnny and we played at The Gibus Club. I played most of the songs on *So Alone*. Johnny was an underground star but he was huge in France. We got treated well each night with bottles of champagne. We all went back to England and a few days later he got deported, so that was that. He came back but we never got a chance to record. The next time I saw him months later we had Lightning Raiders and we opened for him at The Venue in London."

In a tale involving old Hereford friend Peter Farndon, Gass Wild found himself as the original drummer of The Pretenders. "I first met Chrissie Hynde in that same studio where I played with Lemmy," Gass reflects. "She was in a French band at the time so I knew of her. The next time we met was in 1978, after I'd played with Johnny Thunders. I remember being back at the local bar and buzzing because I'd just done these shows with Johnny. Chrissie was there, all depressed.

"So a few months later, I go back to that same bar and the bartender said Chrissie was looking for me. I had no way to reach her but later that day while walking along Ladbrook Grove, I hear a voice shout out the window, 'Hey Gass, come on in!' So Chrissie tells me she's putting a band together and plays me some songs. It turned out Lemmy recommended me to her. She had a rehearsal space so we practiced a few times and it felt great, so then we rehearsed for a month. Then in Easter 1978—I guess I was 26—I was back in Hereford, and I ran into Peter Farndon again. I told him I was working with

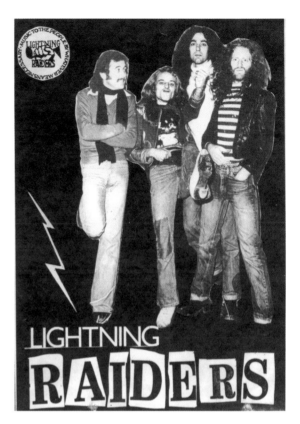

Lightning Raiders band-made flyer, 1978. Designed by Johnny Hodge. Collection of Johnny Hodge

this American girl and it was good stuff. So I got back to London and told Chrissie about my friend Pete who was a great bassist. We all got together and it sounded good, so we rehearsed quite a bit more.

"But she was hard to work with. I knew she was going to make it, she definitely knew what she was doing, but we clashed a bit. And I guess I got fired! Also, she and Pete started having a thing, and I was really upset because I knew that they were gonna make it. At least I was right on that score! But I was pretty broken up about it. In fact, that big black-and-white drum set for Martin Chambers was originally being built for me."

Gass Wild and Chrissie Hynde, *New York Waste*, 2007. Photo by Bruce Alexander. Courtesy of Lucky Lawler.

Gass Wild with Bebe Beull and Taz Marazz, Limelight, New York, 1990. Photo by Norman Blake. Collection of Gass Wild.

After his Pretenders disappointment, Gass ended up back in Paris with a French rock band called The Desperados. That gig steered him to Lightning Raiders.

Gass: "I ran into these French guys in London in early 1980 who'd also contacted me through Lemmy. They said they were playing a week at The Gibus Club where I played with Johnny two years earlier. So we took the hovercraft to France. We played the gigs and then this French label called Underdog said they wanted to put us in the studio. So I ended up being there nine weeks. What started as a couple of songs turned into a 12" EP with five or six songs [1980's *The End Before the Beginning*]. We fired the singer after that week at The Gibus. I told him I wasn't gonna play with him because he embarrassed

me. He thought he was Iggy Pop but he wasn't. I only stayed after they fired him. I told the guys, 'I'll be the singer, let's find a drummer.'

"So after nine weeks in Paris, I wanted to go home. I had nowhere to live and ended up staying with this guy Gordon Hale who managed Lightning Raiders. I played him the tapes we made in Paris. He kept asking me if I played guitar and I kept saying, 'Not well enough to play onstage.' I found out that it was for Lightning Raiders, and I already knew everybody in the band. They were rearranging the Raiders. So in the end they got another lead guitarist with Bruce Irvin, and I joined as the lead singer. We rehearsed for a month and made the first album at The Who's famed studio in South London, Ramport."

Some people still talk about love and peace Try telling that to the police—when they break down your door

— LIGHTNING RAIDERS, "ANOTHER RAID"

THE NEW LIGHTNING RAIDERS, including Gass Wild on vocals, guitarists Johnny Hodge and Bruce Irvine (from Tyla Gang), and Ian Dury/Alex Harvey drummer George Butler, debuted in November 1980 at The Music Machine.

Hodge: "It became a different band. There was nothing left of those folky, hippie roots. It became a full-on hard rock band with a punk edge. The songs with Gass were much more powerful. We kept what worked for this lineup and left out the rest. The songs we wrote are structured, with something mathematical or architectural about them, which is probably why they've aged well. There was a really amazing surge and power of energy when the monster of Lightning Raiders re-entered the room!"

Wild: "Before I joined, Lightning Raiders were a pub band that had done bigger shows with Motörhead. Hawkwind and Pink Fairies were the two great underground rock bands of the time and Sandy played bass in Pink Fairies. The songs I learned when I first joined were the ones Hodge and Allen recorded with Steve Jones and Paul Cook. I was real excited because I knew that I was in a great band. I felt very confident, I thought things were gonna happen."

Hodge: "I hadn't seen Gass since Glastonbury 1971. Then he showed up at my manager's house in London. We formed this group in the summer of 1980 and we made a record and it was great

and we sold it to Island in 1981. So it was a series of coincidences that were destined to happen. It was all so fast. Lightning Raiders only had a year with Gass and I. We worked our asses off, like rehearsing every day for a month. It felt right. So what do you want to know about the catastrophe that beset the Lightning Raiders?"

In 1981, the new lineup made a second Lightning Raiders single, in "Criminal World" b/w "Citizens," and then the *Sweet Revenge* 12" EP—both for manager Gordon Hale's Island Records-distributed Revenge label—co-produced by Hale and Wil Reid-Dick.

Hodge: "What do I remember about making the single? Weak lager and cheap weed, that's what I remember! We were recording the album's backing tracks at Gateway Studios in South West London. We had a list of songs to record, and went through them one-by-one. 'Criminal World,' the single, was just one of the songs we were laying down. At the time of that recording in 1980, there was momentum and excitement. Recording took place in September 1980 and we had the tracks done by mid-December at Ramport."

Wild: "The manager paid for the album, so we approached Island with a finished album. Andrew Lauder signed us. He was no office boy, he was the director of A&R. He loved us after we played at Dingwall's, and within seven weeks we were on Island. We were rehearsing and playing one-off gigs with Motörhead, and then we played Reading. That was fantastic—the biggest gig I've ever done—25,000 people give or take. At Reading, as we were walking off the stage onto the ramp we could hear this mighty roar, like a goal at a soccer match. I just fell against the railing and basked in it. If I never get that again, I got it once. It was absolutely fantastic."

Rock journalist Malcolm Dome raved in *Kerrang!* of a 1981 show in London: "Lightning Raiders melted The Marquee with a fierce display of Southern Fried Acid Metal that Colonel Sanders would have been proud of."

"All the other bands liked us," Wild stresses. "I got to know a lot of these people from other bands when I was in the Raiders. [Blondie drummer] Clem Burke and all of them really liked us, The Stray Cats loved us, I feel that we had integrity."

Lemmy of Motörhead weighs in on the band: "After Gass got a job with the Lightning Raiders as a singer, he really came into himself. I saw them many times. They were great with him. I liked them because they were rock and roll. I like rock and roll and they were definitely a rock and roll band. Remember, that was a time that there were very few rock and roll bands."

The *Sweet Revenge* 12" had a white sleeve with the words, "Pre-Release Limited Edition." No one realized how "limited edition" it would be. Days before Christmas, Island Records decided to drop the band and shelve the album.

Gass Wild: "It was Christmas week that we got the phone call saying Island had dropped us. Johnny was going to Norway to stay with his girlfriend, most of the band was going away. So I said to Gordon, 'Why ruin their Christmas? They're gonna find out when they get back.' I knew but they didn't, and when they found out, I think

they appreciated that. Johnny said he appreciated I didn't ruin his holiday. I went home with a stack of glossy press photos, giving them to nieces and nephews, as well as copies of the EP. I didn't even tell my mother since she was so proud of me. She was a proud mum, she always believed in me. I didn't tell her until I got a new band together. My dad always said I should get a proper job. My mother believed in me as an artist.

"You know, I could understand if they put out the record and gave it a shot and then dropped us. But they didn't even do that. They put out one single that I never heard on the radio. Somebody said they did but I never did. They didn't promote it. We were never given a chance. If they'd given us a chance, we might've made them money and we might be big names now, but we're not. I guess it wasn't in the cards. But we were never given a chance. That's most frustrating about it all."

Island offered no explanation other than telling management that "rock is dead" and that they dropped all of their "rock" bands. But there was another reason: Raiders manager Gordon Hale previously managed new wave one-hit wonders The Jags ("Back of My Hand") and he'd successfully sued Island. As soon as the label figured that out, all ties were severed.

Gass: "Gordon, our manager, had signed a band before he worked with the Raiders called The Jags who had a song 'I've Got Your Number Written on the Back of My Hand.' I never knew what went down but Island engineered the band away from Gordon. He was suing them and they settled out of court. So they were in the wrong. Once they found out Gordon was behind the Raiders, it didn't do us any favors.

"[Island Records owner] Chris Blackwell came back from Nassau where he lived and asked

Gass Wild, Lightning Raiders, Reading Festival, London, 1980.
Collection of Gass Wild.

Their run of bad luck included a big tour that did not happen. Says Hodge, "We had tour support to go on the road with Rose Tattoo. The tour was booked, and all the hotels, and ads ran in the press. It would have been an amazing tour, with a final date at Hammersmith Odeon. But a day or so before it was to start, their singer Angry Anderson got deported back to Australia so that was that. That was part of the downfall. It was such a setback. We didn't have a tour, so we lost momentum, and the label dropped us. Then I lost everything. For a long time I couldn't even listen to those songs. To be that close and then for the thing to fall apart so resolutely was so devastating and heartbreaking. That was the end of Lightning Raiders."

A planned second album, also at Ramport, consisted of two-inch tapes of unfinished backing tracks. The band members couldn't afford to pay the studio around $9,000 after their Island deal imploded and all their assets got seized in Hale's drug bust. Those tapes were never recovered. Gass is certain that they were either disposed of or recorded over.

Hodge: "It was a shame, because we'd done the first album which were songs we'd done all through the Lightning Raiders with Andy. We were doing a second album and we were in the studio for about two weeks. We recorded 13 backing tracks, and it's one of the great lost albums. Our master deck was unpayable because there was no money, the police had confiscated it all. It's a real tragedy. I know that would have propelled the band. We were on fire, and writing some very intense songs. It broke my heart. That summer I worked night after night, crafting these songs I was very proud of."

Andrew Lauder who he'd been signing. They ended up dropping every signing but Peter Shelley. I'm sure all the bands were good—it was a political move. To cap it all, our manager got busted on a coke conspiracy unbeknownst to us. We read about it in the paper. So I had a meeting with Andrew Lauder to tell him what happened to Gordon, and he said, 'Well, I've got bad news too. I've been fired.'"

Gass Wild: "I always wanted a record deal and I got one but I never felt comfortable. It was a major deal—we were on wages and getting equipment and clothes. Everything should've been right but

Gass Wild, with his next band Mannish Boys, Geneva, Switzerland, 1985.
Photo by Jack "Gordo" Lempicki. Collection of Gass Wild.

"The band's collapse in that situation in early 1982 was so complete and fast and total that I had to leave, otherwise I don't know if I could've lived through it. Because of what happened to Lightning Raiders, I had to take a giant step sideways for sanity's sake. I had to put it so far on a backburner—it was too difficult for me. I spent a lot of time in my room, suffering. Then I got married, which really didn't help. It's a rock and roll story."

After Hodge left, the Raiders carried on for a while doing small club shows. "We tried with another guitarist for a while," Gass recalls. "The very last show I did with the band was at Hackney Speedway with Motörhead, Saxon, Angelwitch, and Trust for a Hell's Angels benefit called 'Heavy Metal Goes to the Dogs' [July 25, 1982]. It wasn't the same without Johnny. I mean we played his songs. And the new guy we got, well, he wasn't Johnny. There's a load of guitarists but there's only one Johnny. I mean that.

"The spirit was gone," Gass continues. "The manager went to jail. I got out of the band. I bought a guitar and started practicing every day. Then in 1983 I got Mannish Boys together. First I got this guy Grady who played with Wreckless Eric and was with The Hollywood Brats, who were like the English answer to New York Dolls. He knew the drummer, who knew the bass player. Our first gig was at Bishop's Park in August 1983. The next gig was opening for Hanoi Rocks in Bristol, and a couple more with them. They liked us and were scheduling an upcoming tour and requested us, which was great. So we did a mini-tour, six or seven shows in England, the last one at The Marquee Club was the recording of Hanoi Rocks' 1984 live album *All Those Wasted Years*. Their drummer Razzle called me up the day before he died, saying, 'I'm in LA having a great time…' A few days later my drummer was reading the paper and said, 'Uh, Razzle died in a crash.'"

something wasn't right. All we were trying to do was make the best music, to make them money as well as us. And they made it so hard. It was so devastating. We had an album we were proud of and people dug it. I felt great energy in the studio—the ghost of Keith Moon was rampant. It was an amazing time."

Hodge laughs: "The rate of collapse was very, very rapid. It was looking so great. We had everything going for us. And then it just fell to pieces around Christmas. Within the space of a week my life turned upside down. I left my band, I lost my girl, I lost my flat, I lost my mom. It was awful. My beautiful dancer girlfriend that I loved left me. I lost my flat because the management owned it, and then my mother told me she had terminal cancer. I also had a great publishing deal in the offing. Then it all got ridiculous because of Gordon's legal shenanigans. Looking back, it's not good to think about. It was too devastating. It's part of the tragedy that is Lightning Raiders.

In the night there's a wind of change
Panic at the stock exchange

— LIGHTNING RAIDERS, "ACID COMBAT"

HODGE: "IN THE END, I left the band because there was no more money and I couldn't carry on emotionally. We went from 50 quid a week to 25 quid a week to nothing. That was not gonna work. We had nothing to look forward to. I felt so let down. It's quite awful, actually. It was just rank stupidity by the management. He had a picture of Adolf Hitler on his wall, and he liked us to salute. It was insane, and he insisted on producing. Gass got on with the manager, but the manager didn't understand or even like me very much, even though it was my band and I was the one writing the songs. I was instigating it but at the same time I wasn't someone he could manipulate. Gass feels Gordon helped him develop his voice. As far as I was concerned, he should've gotten on with managing and not sit in the bloody studio and try to produce Lightning Raiders. Wil Reid-Dick worked with Thin Lizzy and was quite an excellent engineer."

Gass carried on with his next band Mannish Boys. After lots of gigging and touring to build a large English and European buzz, the singer set his sights on America.

Wild: "In 1984, Mannish Boys were getting big in the London clubs, building a following. Kids really dug us. Bands like Dogs D'Amour opened up for us. Carol Clark did a piece on us in *Melody Maker* titled 'Ballroom Blitz,' in which Hanoi Rocks also raved about us. I've since heard that many kids looked up to us around Europe. I met kids in Spain who knew more about me than I did! We'd play all around Europe—Norway,

France, Switzerland—and get treated well. In 1985–86, Mannish Boys spent more time playing outside of England than in."

Gass first went to Boston with new girlfriend JoJo Laine, famed groupie ex-wife of Denny Laine (Moody Blues, Paul McCartney's Wings). The rest of the band joined Gass and toured up and down the East Coast, and opened dates for Robert Plant. They recorded a funky rock 12" (one side live plus three studio tracks) with Rolling Stones engineer Jimmy Miller for Motown. That record ran into non-musical problems.

Wild: "In 1986 I met JoJo Laine. We met in London. It was lust at first sight, and then eventually love. We moved to Boston. I came over to visit a few times and liked it. Also, I ran into Jimmy Miller a few years earlier with Lemmy when they were making the *Overkill* album. I met him again when I moved to Boston. We were at The Channel in Boston and I played him our song 'Penetration Sensation' and he loved it. So we talked about him producing. I came back to England, and then he came over and stayed and met the band. I moved in September '86 and the rest of the guys came over before Christmas.

"JoJo and Jimmy went to New York pushing Mannish Boys, to get interest. Jimmy said 'JoJo could sell ice to the Eskimos.' Jimmy got some seed money from Motown Records, of all people, who put us in the studio. We went into Normandy Sound in Rhode Island and cut three songs. We all got $500 for Christmas, which was nice for us all.

Love Pirates, New York, 1991. L-R: Gass Wild, Taz Marazz, Dug Bones, Marky De Sade. Photo by Norman Blake. Collection of Gass Wild.

We carried on gigging and then Motown passed on it. The vice president loved us but the head of marketing told us, 'Sorry, but a white British rock band doesn't fit the Motown model.' So we carried on gigging around the Massachusetts area and some shows in New York. The band broke up when the other guys moved back to England and I stayed. I formed a new Boston lineup of Mannish Boys and then split to LA in November 1987 for seven weeks. Then I had a fight with JoJo and moved to New York. We probably would've killed each other. She believed in me, she loved what I did. But we were both crazy alcoholics. We loved each other but we couldn't live together."

In the late 80s, Gass formed Love Pirates, a bluesy Stones-style band that opened for his friends Hanoi Rocks at The Limelight. "Things just started happening in New York," Gass describes. "I loved being here. I caught the tail end of when New York was still really rocking every night. My first gig here was billed as Gass Wilde & The Toy Bandits and it had Buddy Bowzer who played sax with the Dolls. At that gig I met Dug Bones and we hit it off and decided to put a band together,

and he thought of the name Love Pirates. We rehearsed at The Loft, that famous after-hours club, before the late-night craziness set in. So I jammed there with Axl Rose and Izzy Stradlin, and that was cool because we played on gear with the Love Pirates logo on the drum set. Matt Sorum was still in The Cult when he came. It was a great scene in New York at the time.

"A while after Hanoi Rock's breakup, their bassist Sami Yaffa moved to New York in early 1991. So he joined Love Pirates and we did some recordings with Michael Monroe on harmonica and backing vocals. Then we played The Limelight. First it was Love Pirates with Sami on bass and then Michael joined on vocals for a set of covers dedicated to all our friends who'd died, like Johnny Thunders, Jerry Nolan, Razzle, and Rob Tyner of The MC5."

Regarding Gass' efforts, Lemmy offers the following: "Gass has soldiered on through it all but he hasn't exactly had it easy."

Gass Wild has done a bit of everything. He was an extra in *The Clash of the Titans* and in a Jackie Collins movie. At the time of this writing, he still plays around the city either as Love Pirates or Dirty & Naughty. He has crashed at the same Queens flat since 2003 and pays his bills by painting apartments. Gass lives not as a citizen but as an alien.

"The whole Island Records experience soured me on the music industry," Gass admits. "I love the music and I hate the business. That doesn't mean I wouldn't sign a deal tomorrow if someone offered me one. But I haven't tried to get signed to a major lately. It was soul-destroying, in a way. Everyone dreams of getting a deal, and most people never get that. It makes me more and more determined just to do it well and polish my craft and be as good as I can be. I love playing live and turning people on and making them dance. It's not easy to do that."

Went to a party I didn't stop to think I felt kind of thirsty so I took the nearest drink

— LIGHTNING RAIDERS, "ACID PUNCH"

IN THE 80S HODGE spurned his rock past. "I was really devastated, although I didn't admit to myself what happened to Lightning Raiders. That was six years of my life—my entire rock and roll deal. So in the 80s I got rid of the leather jacket and got into style and clubbing. I went to famous clubs, The Batcave, Hippodrome, and Stringfellow's, and got dressed up and danced. I had a great time, and that went on for years. When it came to wasting my life, I did it with splendor and energy. Going out dancing, going to the raves, became something I did after the Raiders. It's funny, actually, but I had a great time. When things go that badly wrong, you have to forget it. I carried on doing something else. I was getting out of a bad scene with my son's mother and getting off heroin, and was motivated by a need to get on with my life."

He attained cult fame for his wicked role in the 1984 UK hit video for Nik Kershaw's first single, "I Won't Let the Sun Go Down on Me." Hodge recalls that one: "Yeah, that was very funny. Nik Kershaw co-starred in his own video. I was the villain, and it's great to play the villain. I didn't realize until much later that in Sweden that video became very influential there on what'd become the goth scene. It was a great day, filming in some castle in Maidenhead outside London."

Hodge played guitar (credited as "Johnny Dee") on a 1986 album titled *Rocks Off* by the London punk band Chelsea. A decade later he joined the late, great English folk-rocker Bert Jansch's band. Hodge notably wrote the Crowley-infused "La Luna," a highlight of Jansch's final album, 2002's *Edge of a Dream.*

"Working with Bert was great," Hodge recalls. "Then it became not great at all. At one point I never saw him again. It was a great gig but I should've gotten out beforehand. I should've known as soon as Johnny Marr and Bernard Butler and those people started hanging around and I wasn't included that I was no longer on the map. It was quite nasty actually. I was left high and dry again."

"You'd think someone who played with Bert Jansch, Marc Bolan, Steve Jones, and Paul Cook, and all these people, could get a gig. You'd think people would be a little more interested. That's tough, and the idea that they can get you to play for nothing is terrible. But what are you going to do? There are plenty of people willing to play for free or next to nothing. The musician's union doesn't do anything about it. In fact they make it worse. All you can do is wait for another day—which has never arrived."

Gass Wild with Michael Monroe and Sami Yaffa of Hanoi Rocks, Limelight, New York, 1991. Photo by Norman Blake. Collection of Gass Wild.

Paranoia in the village, lines are being drawn
Citizens, which side are you on?

— LIGHTNING RAIDERS, "CITIZENS"

HODGE CAME TO NEW YORK in 2011. He described it as "a dream come true." He hooked up with Gass, who he hadn't seen in 25 years. The two reunited Lightning Raiders with local scene veterans: Tony Mann on drums, guitarist Dominique "Fuz" Larnoy, and bassist Randy Gregg. They rehearsed at John York's studio in The Music Building.

The five-piece took the stage as Lightning Raiders for the first time since 1982. An unadvertised warm-up gig at Otto's Shrunken Head on East 14th Street preceded their official launch at Trash Bar in Brooklyn. During that time, they cut a single in nearby Piermont, New York of "Acid Combat" b/w "Stone by Stone." There was also talk of the new lineup redoing that lost, second Raiders album. As things worked out, there was little interest, so Hodge returned to England. Once again, Lightning Raiders hit a dead end.

"I've known Gass on and off for over 40 years," Hodge ruminates. "It's funny with some people, they're with you for life. I hadn't seen Gass in 25 years—but there's some common bond where you just pick up where you left off. The guy is irrepressible, he's really fantastic. And I know that better now than I knew then."

Soon thereafter, Hodge returned to New York one final time in late 2012 to pursue musical prospects, but things didn't go as planned. A reunion with Liza Todd fizzled. He died in October 2013 at his Camden Town home, of the delitirious effects of his lifestyle.

Hodge: "There's an element of luck in it. We were lucky, but not in a good way. I don't want to rail about old management and partnerships, where I saw people behave in ways that were not at all positive, and it fucks things up. I don't want to go there. You move on. But it's inconceivable how some people can behave. You've got to be thick-skinned to do rock and roll. I think I wasn't able to deal with some of it. I tried to be mean and tough enough. Now, I don't have the time to be messed up by other people."

Gass Wild: "It didn't work out for me. I really thought I was gonna get a deal with The Pretenders, but it didn't happen. Maybe that was my fault. I really clashed with Chrissie. But I carried on—I just have to play. The fact that I haven't made a success of it hasn't stopped me wanting to play, because I love it. There's nothing like playing music and turning people on. I've got no regrets really, though I wish I made more money. I'm not very skilled at anything.

I'm computer illiterate. I didn't graduate—I left school as soon as I was eligible for parole.

"I often think, 'When am I gonna get a break?' That's only natural. I have people that believe in me and I have fans that feel we should be way bigger. I don't see it in the cards yet, but it doesn't make me stop—I'll never stop playing. I'm still ready to rock. I'll rock till I drop. I could be the most jaded person on the planet and I still get excited. There's still a certain amount of magic in music. I love the feeling of playing. It's better than any drug or any woman—it's total mental-physical orgasm. I thrive off it, and that has nothing to do with the business. They can't take that from me. They can never take away the music. I don't consider myself a loser. I'm a winner musically. I've made great music and played with great musicians. Businesswise, I'm a failure—so far." ●

Last known photo of Gass Wild and Johnny Hodge, 179 Stanton Street rooftop. New York, 2011. Photo by Tony Mann.

RICK RIVETS

LR014

Mom, I'm leaving soon
To be the first rock star on the moon

— THE BRATS, "FIRST ROCK STAR ON THE MOON"

RICK RIVETS (George Fedorick) is another New York rock and roll hard luck story. In 1966, the young guitarist, along with a fellow Van Buren High School truant, bassist Arthur "Killer" Kane, played in The London Fogg doing Kinks and Beau Brummels covers. Rivets became acquainted with Johnny Thunders (John Genzale), the guitarist/vocalist of a Rolling Stones-style band, Actress. Rivets and Kane later met David Johansen, a Staten Island-bred Jagger look-alike, at the 1970 premiere of *Beyond the Valley of the Dolls*. Rivets, Kane, Thunders, and Johansen shared a love of trash culture, and so they formed The New York Dolls, adding Rivets' college friend Ken "Sparky" Donovan on drums. After a discordant October 1971 rehearsal, Rivets and Donovan quit the band. Rivets was replaced by Johansen's friend Ronald "Sylvain Sylvain" Mizrahi, Sparky by Sylvain's friend Billy Murcia.

Rivets and Donovan formed a new band, The Brats. The group got its name one night at Max's Kansas City, where Alice Cooper said they looked like a bunch of brats. Their first gig, ironically, was opening for the Dolls at Hotel Diplomat in March 1973. The Brats' colorful frontman Keith West also owned The Music Box, a record shop where KISS hung out. KISS opened for The Brats three times, including in May 1973 at Rivets' Bleecker Street loft for $1 admission. In early

KISS one can hear the influence of Rivets' Anglo-pop proto-metal.

Every major label passed on The Brats' 1973 and 1975 demos. Undaunted, the band released two indie singles: 1974's "Be a Man" b/w "Quaalude Queen" and 1975's "Keep on Doin' (What You're Doin')" b/w "If You Can Rock (You Can Roll)." At Electric Lady Studios they cut "First Rock Star on the Moon" for the ill-fated *Max's Kansas City 1977 (Volume II)* compilation. In 1978, Rivets lost control of his own band, from which he was subsequently fired. The Brats starring Joey Guido carried on sporadically for years, without Rick or Sparky.

Rivets then put together Corpse Grinders with Arthur Kane (fresh from the defunct Dolls), London Fogg singer Stu Wylder, and Teenage Lust drummer Jimmy Criss, all in ghoul makeup. They appeared in October 1977 on Manhattan Cable TV, lip-synching two songs. Corpse Grinders' first live gig was that Halloween at midnight at Great Gildersleeves. Dead Boys guitarist Cheetah Chrome was a fan, and had them play both nights of May 1978's Johnny Blitz benefit at CBGB (Blitz, the former Dead Boys drummer, got stabbed in a bad dope deal). Kane quit after a tepid reception to 1978's "Rites 4 Whites" single deriding minority abuse of public assistance ("*You know*

L: The Brats "Be a Man" b/w "Quaalude Queen" single, Whiplash Records, 1974, Rick Rivets center. Collection of the author.
R: Flyer for The Brats and KISS at Rick Rivets' Bleecker Street loft, New York, June 1, 1973. KISS' first Manhattan show. Collection of Rick Rivets.

I get ever so mean/You tell me that you're part of that welfare scheme!").

Abandoned by his bandmates, Rivets formed The Slugs, a druggy, cocksure, post-Grinders five-piece that at times also gigged as Corpse Grinders. The rude rockers with punk attitude did well, gigging at Max's Kansas City and CBGB, but bad behavior killed industry interest. They acquired a reputation for being drunk, fucked-up, and rude. Nonetheless, they managed to release two singles: 1979's "Problem Child" b/w "Suspicion" and 1980's "I'm in Love with You (Again)" b/w "Never Should Have Told You." Those singles were later reissued stuffed into one sleeve as 1981's *Slugs 2x7.*

The Slugs broke up and Rivets was left high and dry. It was tough for him to watch his peers like the Dolls, KISS, and The Dead Boys achieve greatness while he wallowed in obscurity, a victim of bad attitude, bad vibes, and bad drugs. He had the looks, the chops, and the ambition, but if there was a pattern to his career, it would be that he fell out with his bandmates. He got thrown out of almost every group he formed.

He was never able to get a band together again. But his bad luck extended beyond the musical world. For decades, he has dealt with health issues and homelessness. He occasionally performed with Walter Lure (Heartbreakers/Waldos) as MFU (Martians From Uranus).

Rick Rivets lays out his résumé: "My inspirations were jazz bands. Was in my school band until college, playing drums and trumpet. Picked up guitar in high school and joined bands on bass. The Beatles turned me on to writing originals. Formed New York Dolls with Arthur Kane, my first try at original material. The Brats, started by me and college mate Kenny Donovan gave us a chance to write and release our first records. Still writing and recording for Whiplash Records, started by A.C. Doback and myself in 1975. My goal was always to record and release records." ●

Cherry Vanilla backed by The Police, The Speakeasy, London, 1977. Sting in sunglasses. From *Lick Me: How I Became Cherry Vanilla*. Photo by Ray Stevenson. Special thanks to Ray Stevenson.

CHERRY VANILLA

Black leather jacket and a cycle slut
Big sunglasses and a new haircut

— **CHERRY VANILLA**, "THE PUNK"

CHERRY VANILLA (Katherine Anne Dorritie) was a glitter-rock scene proto-starlet with flaming red hair. She was born October 16, 1943, and grew up in a strict blue-collar Irish Catholic family on Skillman Avenue in Woodside, Queens. Her father was a sanitation man. Her mother worked as a phone operator at the Copacabana, where Kathy got her first taste of nightlife glitz.

"Not that I had a bad childhood, but my dad was Archie Bunker to a T. He was very strict with me. He never hit me but I was afraid of him because he was so fierce—not very logical, kind of stupid. So sometimes I had to escape from him mentally. I had other issues. I was a bedwetter; I had eye operations. So nature was my first escape when my dad humiliated me. Next came show biz. It became my next great escape.

"Even though I was from this Irish middle-class Queens family, which had nothing to do with show biz and stars, I got exposed to it because I'd go in with my father to pick up my mother from work when she got off her shift at the switchboard. He'd take me down to the Copa, and I'd see Jimmy Durante, Martin and Lewis, Eartha Kitt, and all the Copa girls and the band and the booths and palm trees and the cigarette smoke and cocktails—I was in love with it all. It became my new escape; it was my fantasy life. I imagined myself with the Copa girls or the Latin Quarter girls with pink hair and pink costumes or blue hair and blue costumes. In fact, any female role in show biz where they wore skimpy costumes, I was into—legs and color and lights. So, nightclubs became my dream. Maybe not to be a star—although to be a Copa girl would've been okay!"

Kathy's developmental problems caused her parents to brand her a "bad girl"—and so she became one. She got into salty R&B and rock and roll that she heard on the radio. At age 14, she attended her first Broadway play, *Bells Are Ringing* with Julie Holiday. It didn't turn her on like rock and roll did, but that's where she discovered the magic of theater.

Kathy Dorritie and friend, Woodside, Queens, circa 1950. Courtesy of Cherry Vanilla.

station as they played The Flamingos and The Drifters. I'd wait for the DJs to come and go and I'd talk to them and ask them all these questions. That's where my interest in the musical side of show biz began."

She delights in speaking of Murray the K and Allan Freed's rock and roll extravaganzas at the Brooklyn Paramount and the Brooklyn Fox: "It was the tail end of them because I was too young when they first started. I still had to sneak to them; my parents had no idea I was going. I saw Frankie Lyman & The Teenagers, and Buddy Holly, and all these great players. It was so exciting, and for the first time I felt part of something with all these other kids. Your heart started beating to the beat of the music. I knew this was for me, that this was my world. It was the birth of rock and roll and I was a perfect age for it."

Kathy learned to type at All Saints Commercial High School, located among the gutted buildings and vacant lots of 50s Williamsburg. Those office skills led to employment on Madison Avenue during the early 60s when advertising was cool.

"I went to an all-girl Catholic high school where I did some plays—as long as they had costumes or little tutus. I took dance lessons and did recitals. I spent lots of time in my room imagining and dreaming. I was a social kid, but, my father being very strict, I couldn't hang out with boys unless it was a big secret, which made it all the dirtier. As soon as I could, I let a boy stick his fingers up my pussy. I was 11. Then sex started entering the picture.

"I knew I wanted to be in show business, but I was very practical, so I went to a business high school. My parents believed girls didn't go to college. I have a brother and two other sisters

"I got exposed to what they used to call 'race music.' I was seven in 1951, and at that time you could find black stations on the dial. The boys in the streets sang harmonies and started calling it doo-wop, singing it in the public bathrooms of the subways. Then it became known as rhythm and blues. That's still my favorite music. I loved the sexy love songs; Maxine Brown became my favorite singer. So music, not show biz, started taking over. I loved being close to it, being a part of it.

"Listening to the radio became my great escape. It became everything to me. By age 12, I wanted to make contact with the DJs—it wasn't enough just to listen. I wanted to know about them and about the groups they played and how music was made. So I began hanging around this black radio station WWRL that was in Woodside, which had no black people at all. My parents forbade it, but I used to sneak down there and hang around outside. I carried around a big turquoise-and-black Motorola portable radio, and I'd go down there with it and tune in to the and the only one they sent to college was my brother. We were either gonna be a secretary or a nun or get married. So I learned about running an office. I was 17 when I graduated in 1961 and I needed to get an office job. I wanted a show biz-connected office job but I had no idea how to get it."

She got her first job at Sullivan, Stauffer, Colwell & Bayles, a top Madison Avenue agency. "I worked in the TV trafficking department, which in those days meant you organized and sent out the actual films and tapes to radio and TV stations to play. This was real-life *Mad Men*. And the way they treated women was totally that way. Even though I'd been exposed to show biz and rock and roll, the way I was brought up in Queens, I was very naive. But that naivety got me through a lot in life because I never pretended I was smarter or more sophisticated than I was, and people found the honesty refreshing. I think they were taken aback because even though it was hard for women in advertising, I didn't feel that applied to me. Things moved easily for me, it seemed."

By age 19, she was a casting director and producer of commercials at Kastor, Hilton, Chesley, Clifford & Atherton. "It was close enough to show business that I was happy. I was directing people, doing voice-overs, casting, picking production houses and clothing. So I was in show biz, but behind the camera. I liked it, but I have to demystify everything, so I wanted to do something else. I stayed in advertising but sought out other things. But being practical, I always paid my way and paid the rent. I also worked at Bloomingdale's Thursday nights and Saturdays."

Hanging out in Manhattan after work, she got into the Greenwich Village beat culture and the first 60s discotheques like Le Club, Ondine, Arthur, L'Interdit, and the Peppermint Lounge,

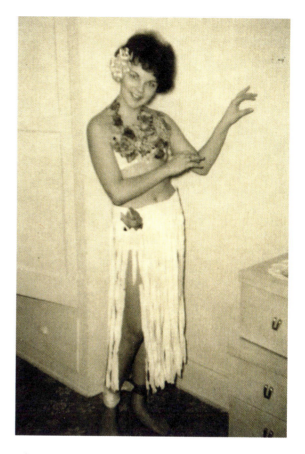

Kathy Dorritie, Woodside, Queens, 1956. From *Lick Me: How I Became Cherry Vanilla*. Courtesy of Cherry Vanilla.

where she got in on the ground floor of the LSD-fueled sexual revolution.

"The first discotheque I ever went to—the first time I ever heard of it—was a little dinner club called Le Club on 55th Street by Sutton Place. The first thing you have to understand is that New York had these weird cabaret laws in those days. I think it had to do with the Mafia and who paid whom. But to get a license allowing people to dance was difficult. People weren't allowed to get up and dance where there were jukeboxes and bands unless the place had a license for it.

This place, the way they got around it, was they called themselves a private club, but I got allowed in somehow. It was a small, intimate French restaurant where you had dinner and a guy played records while you ate and drank. This was something totally different; it wasn't a jukebox or a band. The deejay was known as the *discouier*, playing lovely soft music, a lot of it French. As the dinner ended, the music got more of a beat and louder and people got up on the dancefloor. I immediately loved the idea. Suddenly there was a plethora of these clubs.

"My favorite discotheques were Arthur and Aux Puces. Arthur was on 55th off Third, and Aux Puces was on 55th between Park and Madison. Arthur was larger, but small compared to what discotheques became. Aux Puces was very small; it had a fireplace in the back and chandeliers. It looked like The Casbah. When I hung out at Aux Puces, I got friendly with the DJ, naturally, and he started letting me play during his breaks. That was thrilling and I did for it for free. I started getting free drinks, and I became good friends with the owner Nilo DePaul. He was an amazing character who should have a movie done about him. So I got hired five nights a week to be the DJ at Aux Puces. I was the only female DJ, and it happened organically."

As the 60s evolved from mod to flower power, she got into anti-Vietnam War civil disobedience and peacenik activism. She offered, through her sexual liberation, to "make love not war." Her obsessive-compulsive disorder aided her backstage acumen, making her an amazing groupie and rock and roll scene devotee. She serviced the rock scene under groupie monikers like Party Favor, Indian Summer, Charlotte Russe, Pop Tart, and Thistle Doherty. As a correspondent for an Abbie Hoffman-backed radical pirate radio show, she adopted "Cherry Vanilla" and had no idea that the nickname would stick.

"I had always taken on fantasy names. It was something we'd do when we took LSD, especially. It gave you permission to act in a different way than you normally acted. So you started living out your fantasy life. You could dress or act differently. You could play a character in real life.

"'Cherry Vanilla' came about after I met this guy Richard Skidmore who worked with Abbie Hoffman, and did propaganda tapes for Radio Hanoi. They'd have on the Black Panthers, Weather Underground members, and women's lib activists. So they wanted to do a tape with me. By this time I was a groupie, and he'd spin records by musicians I'd slept with—Burton Cummings, Kris Kristofferson, whoever—and I'd get interviewed and tell stories about them. I never saw how this was a propaganda tape, but they said that it was, and I was all for anything to oppose the Vietnam War.

"They told me to make up a new name for myself, nothing that I'd ever used before, as we could get in trouble. I don't know if there was a yogurt container nearby or if it just popped into my head, but I said, 'Cherry Vanilla.' I was simultaneously writing for rock magazines like *Circus* and *Creem* and *Hit Parader*. I think it was *Creem* first. I had some poetry published as Kathy Dorritie, and then I reviewed the first record by my friend Peter Allen. That's the first time I used Cherry Vanilla in print. The magazine loved it, so I suggested I do a column called 'Cherry Vanilla with Scoops for You'—a rock and roll gossip column. That was my plan. I also wrote pieces for *Penthouse* and *Oui* as Cherry Vanilla because I didn't want my parents to know I was writing for dirty magazines."

Cherry Vanilla, example of her *Creem* magazine advice column, April 1973. Collection of Cherry Vanilla.

America's Only Rock 'n' Roll Magazine

Mick Jagger Dream-Date Winners • Tons of Outrageous Record Reviews

Vol.4 No.11

April 1973
75 Cents

CReeM

Cherry Vanilla ... with scoops for you

Mick Rock

The three essays below constitute the second installment in a continuing CREEM series designed to bring Cherry Vanilla to the world, for which we may or may not be forgiven. For Cherry — poet, author (the soon-to-be published The First Few Days of A Decade — As Seen Through the Eyes of A Tart) musician, narco conjuress, star of stage and screen, world traveller and confidante of the rich, the famous, the beautiful — has been there wherever, whenever the strange changes were going down in the Sixties. Now she is ready to turn and face those of the Seventies, rather than pack all in and hibernate as so many weaker souls have done, and she is also prepared to draw on her wealth of experience to help guide the children of the new age through the gauntlets that await them. You may not know Cherry yet, but rest assured that she knows you; she has been where you and I are, still lives there (at least in the winter months) and her greatest joy is the symbiotic interaction of electric communication at the highest, most basic level. So slide in, pick it up, feed back and Cherry will return the motion and make it all clear. Think of what you are about to read not as "poetry" or "journalism" but as crytstallizations of time and tide, Truth caught and fixed. And remember: her lines are always open. – Ed.

THOUGHTS ON REVOLUTION, LIBERATION, MASTURBATION, ETC.

Never do with your hands what you could do better with your mouth!

SONDRA'S SONG

(Written to a rock star's wife)

My boyfriend is a rock star
and I trust him with my life
He calls me his old lady
That's something like his wife
He goes to California
two, three times a year
I'd like to think he's loyal
but these words my head doth hear:

They may be good at chopping wood
and carrying the load
They may be great at playing mate
but they all mess around on the road

My boyfriend's name is Michael
He's the singer with the band
He also plays piano
and he always holds my hand
He spends his evenings here
except when he's away
I know that he's my honey
but these words my head doth say:

They may be good at chopping wood
and carrying the load
They may be great at playing mate
but they all mess around on the road

So if you've got a lover
who is often out of town
and if his present absence
has got your feelings down
Well just get into your red dress
and stop your being blue
Be happy that you got him
and these words will get you through:

They may be good at chopping wood
and carrying the load
They may be great at playing mate
but they all mess around on the road

SWEET SANE

Some people they like to go out dancing
But Lou Reed
he likes to stay home with me
Some people are into winter prancing
But cold day's coming 'n' you know
where you'll find me
So gay
Oh yeah I'm a rock'n'roll star
So gay
And we know that I'm going far
So gay
But here I sit in my bedroom
Too stoned to even play my guitar
So gay
So gay
Yeah I know I should be working
But I've got to have this time to feel
So gay
Yeah you say and I'm listening
But who really knows what's real
So gay
Yeah I'm gonna paint my face 'cause
There's really nothing else to do
They think I'm a saddened figure
But I'm waiting for the day just like you
I know I'm a little older now
And I guess you know it too
So gay
So gay
So gay
Some people like to run 'round in circles
And others they think
they've found the way
Me I like to play in movies
and live the life
So gay
So gay
So gay
So gay

22

CReeM

Well you can see it when he walks down the alley
He's like a holographic Salvador Dalí

— CHERRY VANILLA, "SO 1950S"

IN 1971, ANDY WARHOL chose Cherry for the lead role in his only play, *Pork*. David Bowie attended the outrageous stage production at The Roundhouse in London, inspiring the balladeer to his bolder Ziggy Stardust persona, which in turn fueled the British glam rock scene.

"This all brings us to the Bowie days when I was in London in 1971 doing *Pork*. The program had me listed as Kathy Dorritie, but it said I was a correspondent for *Circus* and *Creem* under the name Cherry Vanilla. Leee Childers and I were walking to rehearsal for *Pork* at The Roundhouse, and we saw a poster of a guy in a dress: David Bowie. I knew nothing about him but Leee had seen a photo of him in *Rolling Stone* a year or two before. Leee said, 'We gotta go see this guy.' So we went to a club and Jayne County came. It was this little hippie club with people sitting on the floor. We found the woman in charge and it was Angie Bowie and we introduced ourselves. I introduced myself as Cherry Vanilla, which was the first time I ever did that. So we took our place on the floor and she did sound and lights. Angie was one of the first people to never call me Kathy. By that time I was determined to be Cherry Vanilla.

"Several weeks earlier, Dana Gillespie—a girlfriend of David's when he was young who remained friends with he and Angie—a singer, had auditioned to be my understudy in *Pork* and she either didn't get it or didn't take it. But she had the script, so that's how Bowie got ahold of the script and wrote a song for her called 'Andy Warhol.' When he finally did that song it was him on acoustic guitar, Mick Ronson on electric guitar, and Rick Wakeman on piano. His early songs were very Anthony Newley; David was a blend of theater and art rock. He wasn't yet a real rocker. But there were a few new songs that were a bit hard rock and you could tell things were developing. At the show when he got to 'Andy Warhol' he said there were people from the Warhol play and asked us to take a bow. In *Pork*, one of my signature moves was I kept popping a tit out of my shirt. He presented me as Cherry Vanilla and I popped out my tit. So that's the first glimpse David Bowie ever had of me. Of course we all hung out after the show.

"Jayne County will tell you David was a hippie before he met her and saw *Pork*, but I don't see it that way. Bowie, even earlier in his career, had shorter hair and wore leather jackets. He was just in his longhaired Veronica Lake phase when we met him. I'm sure we had an influence because he loved Warhol and we were his representatives. But I don't think we changed his life. I feel Angie and Mick Ronson were bigger influences; Angie found the right people for the costumes and hair, and Mick influenced David toward the harder sound you heard on *Ziggy Stardust*."

Cherry and Angie turned David Bowie onto the decadent New York nightlife of Max's Kansas

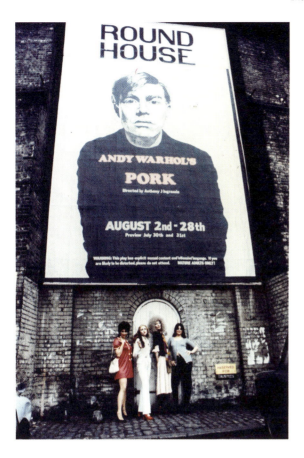

Cherry Vanilla with the cast of *Pork*, The Roundhouse, London, August 1971.
Photo by Leee Black Childers. Courtesy of Leee Black Childers.

City, Club 82, Mercer Arts Center, and other late-night hotspots. The ladies also introduced him to Andy Warhol.

"I first went to Max's Kansas City when I was in advertising with Paul McGregor the hairdresser, a good friend of mine who did that famous Jane Fonda shag haircut in *Klute*. He took me there for dinner in the front, and told me about the artists who hung out in the back. The place had cheap surf-and-turf and a great jukebox, so I started going there for dinner. When you went to the ladies room, you could peek into the back room,

and it all looked very intimidating. They looked up when you went to the ladies room because they checked everybody out.

"Funny enough, when I was doing Theater of the Ridiculous I met all those people: Tony Zanetta, Wayne County. One night they said we should go over to Max's, and they walked right into the back room because they were part of it, and I walked in with them. That was my entry. Once I had that, I was in—I was part of the back room. Warhol sat at the back corner table, and I only sat there a few times. I think you could sit eight people around that table.

"When I auditioned for Andy, that was super-anointing because he was famous and the hippest artist on the scene. He was *it* in our eyes. And to me, what he did with his art was much like the advertising world I came out of. It was advertising as art. Andy was a revelation. So getting chosen by him for the lead role in his only play was holy. It was like, 'I'm an Andy Warhol super-star! I am art. I am living art. I'm anointed by Andy, he chose me, he asked for me.' So that was heavy. Then the fascination and ego boost goes away and you get down to work and you realize, 'Oh God, I'm on every page of the script with this speed-freak dialogue, and I've never done anything like this before. Can I handle this? Am I talented enough?' Then it just becomes part of the fabric of who you are.

"Being part of the Warhol scene was the same feeling I got when I first went to the rock and roll shows at the Brooklyn Fox and Paramount. There was a feeling of strength in numbers and being part of a movement. So being involved with that clique or in-crowd—it boosted your bravery and ego, you felt like you were with the cool kids. You had no fear because you had these other folks behind you. It gave me confidence and belief, and a confirmation of my talents. It didn't really change me at the core as a person, but people definitely did begin to treat me differently.

"But like all things in life, you take it in stride. It was a special thing. I knew then that one day I'd be writing my life story because I was connected with Andy. No one could take that away from me. Whether the play was a hit or a flop, whether I was good or bad, I was connected with Andy Warhol. And because we traveled *en masse* and were Warholian, people paid attention. So we played it for all it was worth. We were loud and naughty. We'd jump on the bars and dance and have sex in the bathrooms, and they tolerated it. To young, artistic, edgy, underground people, we were a hit. That was cool."

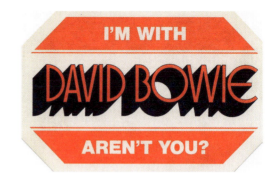

David Bowie sticker, 1972. Concept by Cherry Vanilla. Collection of Cherry Vanilla.

He took me for a ride but I'm in love with him still
He snorted forty grams of coke and I'm still paying the bill

— CHERRY VANILLA, "HARD AS A ROCK"

"DAVID AND HIS MANAGER Tony DeFreis wanted to come to America, and they saw in us the chance to connect them to Warhol's crowd. After *Pork* they traveled to New York a lot to get David signed to RCA. Leee and I would attend these meetings with Tony at the Warwick Hotel, where he'd stay when in town. For dinner and drinks we'd tell him everything we knew, and introduce him to the promoters and radio DJs, and rock journalists and photographers. He was using us in a way, but we didn't care. We felt great that we could provide such advice. Then he began taking us up to RCA as a diversion as

he manipulated them to get more money. He was a very clever man. We loved it because we were Tony's little advisors but we knew nothing about the record industry. That was great because we'd ask for things no one ever asked for. We didn't care who we insulted because we didn't have a job.

"In early 1972, I got a call from Tony Zanetta, who was running MainMan America from a duplex on 58th Street, needing someone to answer the phones. He hired Cyrinda Foxe, but she couldn't handle it. The first day I got there, there was

Cherry Vanilla, the star of Andy Warhol's only play, *Pork*. The Roundhouse, London, August 1971. Photo by Leee Black Childers. Courtesy of Leee Black Childers.

a table, some phones, maybe a few glasses and cups, and a teapot. Bowie was coming to the States to start his tour and I saw they were in trouble. Since I had a background with ad agencies, I was the only one who could get the whole thing together. So I got file cabinets and typewriters and dry cleaning and limo accounts. I was the only one who could type, so I'd type up contracts. It was an amazing challenge, and I loved it. It was rock and roll management, but I could use every skill I'd learned before to do it. It was great because I was good at it, even though I was delving into an area I knew nothing about—making it up as I went along, which was great cause I knew nothing about rules or courtesies or unions. I did things as I saw fit.

"Tony DeFries had this rule that we weren't going to let Bowie speak to the press, even though he wasn't even in demand yet. So I told writers, 'You can't speak to Bowie but I'm his spokesperson so you can talk to me.' But I really didn't know much about him before *Hunky Dory*. So I'd just say anything. When they asked, 'What was the Third Bardo?' I'd say, 'Oh, Bowie loves Brigitte Bardot.' I'd just say whatever was at the top of my head. I loved talking to the press. It made me feel important. I loved to make up stories and act clued-in. I had such freedom. I'd go on the radio stoned out of my head and say whatever popped into my head. Everyone thought David was gay, so I'd do interviews talking about what a great fuck he was and really confuse people. That was my PR plan, because the rock stars I wanted to fuck were the records I'd buy. And we sold out all the halls.

"I helped set up his first real New York show at Carnegie Hall. I was in the front row with Angie screaming 'Suffragette City!' He was an instant hit. Of course we primed the pump for him to become a hit. We had all our journalist friends from Max's there and all our Warholian friends and all our contacts in radio and advertising. We primed it, but he had to live up to it, and he really did—he was fantastic. It was then I started dyeing my hair red. I was wearing tons of makeup and my PR lady costumes with 40s-style dresses and jackets, high heels and garter belts. Then I knew I was Cherry Vanilla. While I worked for Bowie during this incredible time, I knew I was no longer Kathy Dorritie."

Cherry told John Lombardi at the *Voice* (6/30/75): "Listen, we peddled David's ass like Nathan's peddles hot dogs. When I first met him, David was butch; he was into his wife Angela. In 1970 I was in England doing Andy's play *Pork*; nothing had happened in terms of gayness. We went in with all these screamer queens, and the English—they're quite sweet, they didn't know what was going on. They thought America was like *Pork*—hah! We told David and his manager Tony DeFries that David could be the biggest star in the world. Of course we didn't know if we were right. We were just bullshitting. But bullshit works. I used to work in advertising. RCA went for a huge publicity push, a fat contract—it was terrific. On the *Diamond Dogs* tour we traveled first class and ran up a $400,000 tab. If American kids weren't into gayness before the tour, they were into it when we finished. And RCA was responsible—hah!"

Cherry fell out with MainMan after she expanded her role at that company by running an in-house production team for photo shoots and videos. The final straw was an unreleasable concert film by Bowie guitarist Mick Ronson made to coincide with the release of his 1974 solo album *Slaughter on Tenth Avenue*. The film, to be called *Live at the Rainbow*, was in debt $60,000, prompting DeFries to pull the plug.

Her lofty dreams of rock business success suddenly went down in flames. She saw her role with Bowie was as an agitator and renegade. Such status generally was not respected by the industry. She knew that she was a bit too old to return to servicing the scene as a groupie, so she considered her own artistic possibilities: "A lot of people ask how I made the transition from rock and roll PR lady to pop star. When I got fired from MainMan, after I was a PR lady, I felt like Bowie had achieved a certain level, and I was more interested in film. Then they asked me back, but I couldn't go back to PR because there were already new people I had hired, and I didn't want to go back to that. Tony offered me a role as a MainMan artist but he wanted to own everything past, present, and future, and I couldn't do that either."

Cherry Vanilla, New York, 1978. Photo by Leee Black Childers. Courtesy of Leee Black Childers.

Careful now don't give your love for free
Or you may turn out a bad girl like me

— CHERRY VANILLA, "BAD GIRL"

"A GOOD GROUPIE should keep her mouth shut. A publicist wants to talk about it all. In a way, I was a good groupie and a good publicist because I'm only recently, 40 years later, talking about who I slept with. A lot of it I couldn't talk about. When I wrote in *Penthouse*, it was under different names. In PR, you have to get to people that a lot of people are trying to get to, and you have to get their attention, and you have to have something interesting to say or an interesting product to sell.

So in a way it's alike because that's part of the victory that comes with being a groupie, that you could get to people—in bed or close-up— that others only wished they could. As a publicist you have to be able to get to the journalists and TV newspeople you want. You don't use

anything, you've gotta use your noodle and work really hard.

"I talk to people today and they think it was so glamorous, just partying and fucking all the time. Yeah, that was the part we showed everyone, but we were in the office at two in the morning or seven in the morning or whatever it took. My mother gave me a great work ethic. I mean, even after I was a pop star, I did plenty of menial work, and I did it the best that I could because I had to earn a living."

Cherry's next step to becoming a musician was offbeat poetry, leading to comedy/cabaret: "I Xeroxed 50 copies of everything in my notebook about rock star fucking and other groupie stuff. I gave these poems away as Christmas presents. They were a big hit with my friends, who said I should do a book. So I did a little poetry and picture book. That led to my new company out of my loft, Vanilla Productions. To promote the book in October 1974, I decided to perform the poems in the book. It was upstairs at Ritazzi's, a restaurant we used to go to when I worked on Madison Avenue (it got mentioned in *Mad Men*). It was the first time I ever did my own poetry. In theater, it was just reciting others' lines. It was a big hit and I sold lots of books. Finally I had a way to promote my product.

"Reno Sweeney was the big cabaret of the day, and I used to hang out there. I knew the owner so I auditioned for him, even though I didn't know what the hell my act was. But most of my poems were kind of funny. Lots of it was about behind-the-scenes rock and roll. He offered to book me and asked me how many songs I had, and I knew I had none. So I found this 17-year-old pianist/composer and bathhouse denizen, David Schaefer. In those few weeks between the audition and the gig, we wrote three comedic songs. So I got booked there for a week as Holly

Cherry Vanilla, New York, New Year's Eve 1975. Photo by Leee Black Childers. Courtesy of Leee Black Childers.

sex like you do as a groupie, but even being a groupie you don't just use sex, you have to be very clever to get close to these people. Then you can use sex to get them into bed—but you have to be clever. In that sense, the skills are similar. I don't think there are many dumb groupies. I haven't met one. Pamela Des Barres is brilliant. Cynthia Plaster Caster's no dummy— she knew what she was doing. But it's like

Woodlawn's opening act. I did my act and people were rolling in the aisles. During that week of shows, David Bowie and Mick Jagger came. So that got in the papers and word got around.

"I was getting booked all over as this cabaret, comedian, poet—whatever—and I got write-ups you wouldn't believe. Rock musicians wanted to come accompany me. So I started writing songs and trying to sing them the best that I could. Then it occurred to me, 'Where do I go from here?' I loved my act, but I loved rock and roll more. David Schaefer didn't know how to write rock, so I went to my pal Michael Kamen, but he was transitioning from New York Rock & Roll Ensemble to soundtracks and ballets."

Then, as if by magic, she heard from her fellow groupie friend Nancy Andrews, who was living in Tulsa with Carl Radell, formerly of Derek and the Dominos and performing in Leon Russell's band. Nancy suggested that she work with Patrick Henderson, a former Texas church reverend playing piano with Leon.

"I got on a plane to Tulsa and I had these poems. In 72 hours, Patrick turned ten of my poems into songs. He was so fast—and good songs. We went to Leon Russell's studio and recorded them on his grand piano. We brought Patrick Henderson to New York and he lived at Max's and played as my musical director. Mick Ronson helped me find my first band, and they were

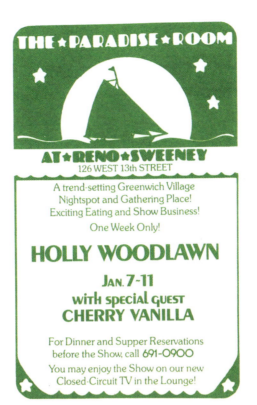

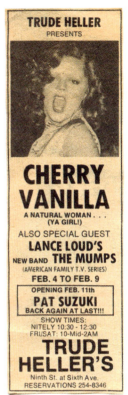

L: Cherry Vanilla opening for Holly Woodlawn at Reno Sweeney, 1975.
R: Headlining over The Mumps at Trude Heller's, 1976. Collection of Cherry Vanilla.

fantastic musicians. So even though I wasn't the best singer yet, I had the personality going, I had the songs, and I had great musicians. I began getting booked at rock clubs, and that's where it went. The next step was getting a record deal.

"Bowie had always been saying that he wanted to make a record with me. He was just starting to delve into electronic music with synthesizers, and he wanted to do synthesizer music that I'd do poetry over, and call it The Electric Beatnik.

That probably would've been a good idea had I followed through. But Bowie's synthesizer music at that time was very primitive. He was like doing imitations of pop songs on synthesizer; it sounded corny in a way. Sure I wanted to work with Bowie, but I also wanted to rock, stripped down rock and roll, punk rock."

I was singing blues and I was rocking as well And the atmosphere was so out of sight

— **CHERRY VANILLA, "LIVERPOOL"**

IN LATE 1975, Cherry made her first attempt at being a rock star. She performed at Max's as part of the embryonic Downtown punk scene. Her first release, "Shake Your Ashes," appeared on 1976's *Live at Max's Kansas City* compilation. Everyone involved thought the album was going to be huge. It was not, but it became influential on a cult level. Then she moved to London with *Pork* cohorts Wayne County and Leee Childers to partake in the 1977 UK punk explosion.

"So I'm in New York and punk rock's happening. I've got a band playing all the clubs, getting lots of publicity. The band was changing all the time and it was making me crazy. I had become like a casting director for rock musicians. I had Kasim Sultan in my band and then Todd Rundgren comes to one of my gigs and offers him more money, so there goes Kasim. I understood, but it was very difficult. The money we were paying

Top: Cherry Vanilla with Mick Ronson, 1973. Photo by Leee Black Childers; Bottom: *Live at Max's Kansas City* compilation, RAM Records, 1976. Collection of the author.

Cherry Vanilla Band, Club 82, New York, 1975. From *New York Rocker*, 1976. Photo by Lee Black Childers. Collection of Cherry Vanilla.

the rehearsal studios ate up anything we made at the gigs, and then someone would quit and you'd have to start all over again. At one point I started billing my band as 'Cherry Vanilla & This Week's Band' because that's what it was. My bands came and went.

"Suddenly I had all these guys from Staten Island, so I started calling it 'Cherry Vanilla & The Staten Island Band.' With guitarist Thomas Moringello I wrote 'Shake Your Ashes.' We cut it

in a studio in Stockbridge, Massachusetts that'd just had a fire, so we got it very cheap or for free. Then I did demos for a few producers. But I didn't record anything else until I went to London and did 'The Punk.'

"I was jealous of Debbie Harry and Patti Smith, that they had musicians who seemed so devoted to them. I didn't feel mine were. Mine were using me but I was using them, too. They knew I could get booked and get press exposure, and

Cherry Vanilla, "The Punk" single, RCA UK, 1977. Photo by Matthew Rolston. Collection of the author.

Cherry Vanilla with her guitarist Louie Lepore, London, 1979. Photo by Willie Christie. Collection of Cherry Vanilla.

people seemed to like me, but I never felt my band members liked me too much. They wanted a great singer, and they were kind of jealous of me, that I got all the press and interviews and photos taken. So it was a funny relationship. But while I was insecure, there was nothing I could do but push forward. I had to keep learning, I had to keep earning, and I had to get that record deal."

Deborah Harry, Patti Smith, and Cherry Vanilla had all performed in off-Broadway theater and other low-budget productions together. "I'd done a play called *Island* with Patti Smith, and I did a play with Debbie Harry called *Victory*. In stage and theater, everyone's so giving to each other because everyone has to be good—otherwise the ship goes down. So you're not trying to outdo your fellow actor, you're trying to get the most out of them so that it works as a whole. It is a strength-in-numbers thing. We knew punk was stronger as a movement. It kind of started with the Ramones.

They were the first band I remember being called punk. It gave an outlet to all these garage bands, and we were all pop/garage bands. Now we were all part of this 'death to disco, we want rock, back to the basics!'

"I saw punk as one big theater piece that we were all a part of. We all hung out at Max's. We went to parties together. We helped each other with equipment. Debbie Harry may have been the only person we knew in Manhattan with a car. She used to give people rides to the gigs, and put their drums in the trunk. People helped each other. When I got a gig I'd get my friends to play the opening slot, and other people did the same for me. There was of course some rivalry—but it was a healthy rivalry. People always said Blondie's 'Rip Her to Shreds' was about me. But Debbie said that it wasn't about me, it was about this waitress at Max's. But if it was about me, I'm flattered. It's a great song."

I'm waitin' like hell for my little red rooster to come back to town
You know he said he'd produce, produce a record for me

— CHERRY VANILLA, "LITTLE RED ROOSTER"

"MILES COPELAND WAS at one of our gigs in New York, at this basement club called On the Rocks. After the gig he said if we ever made it to England he could get us bookings. There was always a desire to go to England because it was the center of this punk explosion, and Carnaby Street and Merseybeat were romantic to us rock and rollers. Leee Childers was in England with Johnny Thunders and the Heartbreakers and they were on tour with the Sex Pistols, and Leee started calling me incessantly. He said, 'It's history going on over here, you have to come and be part of this history…' So it was in the back of my mind. Then I was walking into Max's to go to the back room and 'Anarchy in the U.K.' came on. It cut through from the speakers like nothing else I'd ever heard. I stopped dead in my tracks and said, 'What is this?' I asked around and they said it was the Sex Pistols. 'That's the Sex Pistols? Leee is on tour with the Sex Pistols and Johnny Thunders. I'm going to London—that's it, I'm going.'

"So I told Miles Copeland I had enough money to bring over Zecca my keyboardist and my guitarist Louie Lepore, who was now my boyfriend. Miles said, 'That's great because my brother has this little band and they can't get any bookings because they've got no PR hooks.' I had the PR hooks with Warhol and Bowie, so I could get press and get gigs. His brother's band was The Police. So he said, 'You can travel in one van and share one set of gear and they'll play bass and drums for you, and this way we can make it work.' So we went to England and met The Police before they had Andy Summers. We worked out this deal for them to be my band, at least the rhythm section of Stewart Copeland and Sting. I paid them ten pounds each a night, which was about $15 then. That meant Louie and Zecca sometimes got no pay. Most of the time we slept on people's floors after shows. That led to playing all over England and Europe with them. I began getting record offers, as did The Police."

That group was the original Police lineup of Stewart Copeland (drums), Henry Padovani (guitar) and Gordon "Sting" Sumner (bass). They were promoting their first self-released single, 1977's "Fall Out" b/w "Nothing Achieving." Cherry Vanilla and The Police toured Europe, and everything went great until she got pregnant. She took a few weeks off the tour to exercise her reproductive rights. Cherry never caught up with The Police, who kept on touring, so when the trauma subsided, she brought over more New York musicians.

"I'd gotten pregnant accidentally. Louie was only 21 years old and he freaked out. He was not gonna have a baby, he was not gonna be a father, and he was gonna leave me and not play in my band or anything if I was gonna have this baby. Plus I was taking all these drugs and had no money. So

  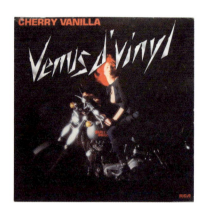

Cherry Vanilla on RCA UK: *Bad Girl*, 1978. Photo by Matthew Rolston; *Liverpool*, 1978. Photo by Matthew Rolston; *Venus D Vinyl*, 1979. Photo by Willie Christie. Collection of the author.

although we didn't end our relationship, it changed things, because I would've had that baby come hell or high water. Then I started having doubts about Louie as a boyfriend because I was 34 years old at the time. It was a tough time emotionally. OK, you're young, you've got a million excuses, you're on the road with a rock band, you're not gonna get a record deal if you're pregnant. Being the practical person I am, you make these decisions, have an abortion and move on, like it was nothing, and go back to work. But it wasn't nothing. And revisiting these buried feelings really hurts."

After a gig at The Nashville, CBS made an offer that Cherry accepted. But there were other interested parties. A bloke named Andrew Hoy worked in the RCA UK press office back when Cherry did PR for Bowie. By 1977, he'd moved up the ladder to be an A&R agent. Hoping to turn Cherry into a star, Hoy went to one of Cherry's gigs at The Nashville with a few RCA execs who liked what they heard. The project was approved.

"I signed to RCA and gave CBS their money back. We recorded at Air Studios in London, which was where The Beatles and George Martin had worked. Phil McDonald, our engineer, had

worked with The Beatles. I made Andrew Hoy our producer. He'd only produced demos before that, but I liked his sound because it sounded big. I liked it and loved him because he was my friend. Phil was an alcoholic at the time and when he drank I sometimes felt nasty vibes. Another thing was I always used to perform stoned and weed was my thing, and it was not easy to find it in England at the time. You could get hash but it wasn't the same, plus people mixed it with tobacco and I never smoked tobacco. I'd smoke it, just to get high on something, and the tobacco made me sick. And my band at the time included my boyfriend, so they were always very critical. I wanted some criticism, but it often crossed a line because I needed some ego to really sing. So that was traumatic, but I got through the recording.

"I was happy with the album but then came the marketing problems. I probably should've been on a smaller label better able to cater to the punk market. The worst part that happened was they had a planned release date for September and then Elvis Presley died, so my release date kept getting pushed back because all the pressing plants were booked printing Elvis records. That was a bit funny, all of our timing got changed.

"I don't know how much I wanted a recording career as much as I wanted a hit record that would give me money for the rest of my life. I was very practical about it all. I didn't know how long I wanted to be a rock star per se—all the makeup, costuming, and whatnot, and dealing with all the attacks in *NME* or whatever. But I wanted a hit record or a couple of hits because when I grew up, I knew that there were people who had made one hit record in the 60s and they were living off it for years. That doesn't happen anymore, but I felt I had to get a hit record, and I thought 'The Punk' was a hit. It was a pop record but it was all about punk. I could blame RCA but maybe it just wasn't good enough. I guess I'll never know. It was a hit in Holland; it got some airplay."

Paradoxically, her worst moment came when she got an offer from Robert Stigwood, mega in the 70s with The Bee Gees and *Saturday Night Fever* and RSO Records. He was ready to do something big with "The Punk." It was a missed opportunity from which her career would never rebound: "Robert was hot on the song, and wanted to put it out in America. And he would've done great with it because he was all about show biz and he probably would've turned 'The Punk' into a Broadway play. So this man Peter Bailey, head of business affairs at RCA UK, flew over to the US to meet Robert Stigwood and make the deal. And when Peter Bailey came back he said no deal because RCA UK had first-rights for the rest of the world, and they were going to put it out worldwide. But that never happened; they kept pushing back the US release. I went to Glen Clancy, the label's president, and cried to get off the label. I said, 'Please let me off while I still have a chance...' and they wouldn't let me off. Because of that, I lost that moment with Robert Stigwood."

Her New York crew, including Louie Lepore, played on two Andrew Hoy/David Stratten-co-produced albums for RCA UK: 1978's *Bad Girl* and 1979's *Venus*

Cherry Vanilla press shot for RCA UK, 1978. Photo by Matthew Rolston. Collection of Cherry Vanilla.

D'Vinyl. Both failed to connect with consumers: too offbeat for pop, too old-school for punk. The British press, who adored her in the Warhol and Bowie days, turned merciless toward her music.

"Louie and I stayed in England for a while and wrote romantic songs. That was *Venus D'Vinyl*. We were trying to expand and see if I could sing those kinds of songs. RCA did nothing with it and it was over. I was done. I had enough of the rock star game. It was no panacea. That thing of people looking at you when you walk into the room and getting all the attention—I wasn't even sure if I wanted that anymore. Because with that comes all these responsibilities. You better not get old, you better not get fat, you better not get wrinkles, you better be wearing designer clothes. So I was ready to go a bit more underground again. Louie and I tried one last time with a theatrical act mixing rock and cabaret, which we described as "Caba-Wave."

"While at RCA I met composer Vangelis and he was attracted to me right away, and he pushed me to leave Louie. So he kept on hammering away because he wanted me, but we were just friends at that time. So Louie and I went back to America and lived together for a while, and then he cheated on me. So I broke up with Louie and stopped doing music. I wrote a lot for magazines to make a living. Then I briefly married a German actor. I did reunion gigs with the band for fun but that was the end of my music career.

"I hid it all from my parents. Many years later, I was playing at this club SNAFU—this was after I came back from London—and I invited my parents. It was the first time they came to see me. I was doing songs like 'Hard as a Rock' and 'Foxy Bitch,' but my parents loved show biz so much, suddenly it was okay and they thought it was great. I'm so glad they got to see me before they passed. But I knew I had to keep it secret from them until they could finally accept it."

Cherry Vanilla Band, 1975. Photos by Leee Black Childers. Collection of Cherry Vanilla.

Some people hate me for the opportunities I took Well I ain't never hurt nobody I just know how to hook

— CHERRY VANILLA, "I KNOW HOW TO HOOK"

CHERRY'S QUEST for rock stardom fizzled. After all the promises that never materialized, she spent the next decade or so licking her wounds.

During that time she aged out of being a sexy rock harlot.

In the early 90s she provided orgasmic vocals on dance 12"s credited to she and house music legend Man Parrish, including 1992's "Techno Sex" and "Fone Sex." After that, she moved to Hollywood to run her old suitor Vangelis' American publishing company. She was thrilled to be back in the business of music.

Over time, her fabulous lifestyle gave way to normalcy and dealing with real-life issues like the demise of her aging parents. She moved back to Queens and back into the familial fold, but then fell out with her siblings, losing her share of the family home, leading to destitution before rebounding to functionality. She dealt with mental problems. Her overwhelming regret is not having saved money for retirement.

"What I wanted at different stages of my life have been different—but one thing I've always wanted was to be involved with show biz. And because of working with Vangelis and writing a book, I still am. But if I wrote a second book it'd be a much heavier trip. It would be about mental breakdowns and taking Prozac and having OCD to the max and suffering from depression and being homeless. But here I am, with a happy ending!"

Cherry had her share of bad luck and missed opportunities but her "lost" status had nothing to do with lack of connections or lack of commitment. Cherry knew what she wanted and she knew how to get it. Yet she could never capitalize on her business savvy, despite direct links to Warhol, Bowie, Jagger, and the glam and punk explosions. Maybe it was the blowback of being a brassy Queens broad in the male-dominated rock industry. Maybe her groupie legacy caused others to not respect for

her art. Maybe Cherry was just too Warholian for the real world.

Cherry's longtime industry-veteran friend Michael Alago put it succinctly; "Cherry is such an incredible woman. She's fun, she's sexy, and she worked really hard back in the day. We all know of her 70s days as a groupie, her ties to Warhol and to Bowie, who was already a big star. Cherry was reading poetry and writing books. She didn't have a great voice but she was so charismatic and sexy. Yet despite all that, and a major label contract, it just never clicked. Even after all these years I have no idea why it doesn't connect." ●

Cherry Vanilla, Los Angeles, 2010. Photo by Arlene Pachasa. Collection of Cherry Vanilla.

LR016

ROBERT FLEISCHMAN

Wheel in the sky keeps on turnin'
I don't know where I'll be tomorrow

ROBERT FLEISCHMAN grew up in Torrance, California with rock star aspirations. Early in his life, it was evident that he had a great voice. An early job took him to Chicago, where concert promoter Barry Fey heard his demo and got him signed to CBS. The label's bigwigs were lukewarm on the songs but needed a great pop singer for their critically acclaimed jazz-fusion supergroup Journey.

So from June through October 1977 Fleischman was Journey's lead singer. He never performed live with them but for 1978's multi-platinum *Infinity* album he co-wrote the FM classics "Any Time," "Winds of March," and "Wheel in the Sky." For the latter he reworked bassist Ross Valory's wife Diane Valory's poem "Wheels in My Mind." Fleischman already had a manager, and butted heads over that fact with Journey's manager Herbie Herbert, who spitefully replaced Fleischman with Steve Perry. The rest is history.

Falling out with Journey was a major disappointment. But within weeks, he signed with Clive Davis at Arista. Future hit-maker Jimmy Iovine over-produced Fleischman's 1979 LP *Perfect Stranger*. To promote the record, the singer toured three months opening for Boston, Eddie Money, and Van Halen. Fleischman speaks disparagingly of Iovine for spending and taking more than his fair share. The record flopped and the tours made little impact, and Fleischman took it hard.

In 1982 Fleischman rejected an offer by Geffen A&R man John Kolodner to replace John Wetton on vocals in the British prog-pop supergroup Asia because he knew, probably correctly, that he was not the right man for that job. Another setback came two years later, when he recorded for Epic with the short-lived, melodic hard rock group Channel, a train wreck produced by L. Ron Hubbard's son-in-law John Ryan. The ordeal led to the group's disbandment within months of the album's release.

Fleischman had previously sung on a rejected demo for a band with guitarist Vinnie Vincent before he joined KISS. After Vinnie's KISS stint ended in 1984 he called upon Fleischman to be the

Vinnie Vincent Invasion, Los Angeles, 1986. Robert Fleischman, top;
Vinnie Vincent, bottom. Chrysalis Records publicity photo by Moshe Brakha.
Courtesy of Robert Fleischman.

singer on 1986's *Vinnie Vincent Invasion* (Chrysalis), an over-the-top metal opus that must be heard to be believed. The album included an airbrushed cover shot of Robert with short hair and a riding crop. The singer claims he got ambushed at the photo shoot for his unexpected fashion make-over, and still cringes over the experience.

Fleischman hated everything about that album: the fights with the engineer, the vocal booths lined with *Playboy* centerfolds for "inspiration," Vinnie's unhinged solos, and various other *Spinal Tap*-isms. When the singer wouldn't sign a 200-page contract for zero money, Chrysalis threatened to strike his vocals from the record. But they did something worse: they hired Mark Slaughter (later of Slaughter), who wore lingerie panties over his acid-washed jeans as he lip-synced to Robert's vocals on the group's

MTV video, "Boys Are Gonna Rock" (and sang on 1988's follow-up *All Systems Go*). Fleischman successfully sued Chrysalis, but the entire episode was a disaster.

Despite that fiasco, Robert tried one final time with Vinnie Vincent in 1989, incredibly agreeing to work on a third VVI album for the punk label Epitaph. But Vinnie ruined that deal, too. Excited by his new tunes, Vinnie began contacting major labels for a better deal. Epitaph felt double-crossed after laying out lots of studio money, so that was that. (Some of those songs made Vinnie Vincent's 1996 *Euphoria*.)

Robert Fleischman spent most of the 90s and 00s raising a family, painting in his spare time, making indie records, and singing for commercials. He sang with Journey (*sans* Steve Perry) at their 2005 Hollywood Walk of Fame ceremonies. After that event, one-time VVI drummer Andre LaBelle reached out, and the two decided to form a pop-rock act. Strong rehearsals in Richmond convinced Robert to relocate his family to Virginia in order to play as The Sky and record 2011's *The Sky* for managers Winogradsky/Sobel's Win/So label. Neither that, nor 2014's *Majestic*, nor 2015's *Stratosphere* tore up the charts.

He is haunted by what could've been. That pot of gold was so close that he could almost feel it. Yet he maintains an undying hunger, and would do most of it all over again. "People always tried to put me in different bands, trying to fit a square peg in a round hole. They even tried to put me in the group Kansas! It was that instant-formula crap. I wish I got back on the bike but I stayed off longer than I should have. I should've been playing and writing but after a while it gets bombastic. I got to climb the ladder, but then I climbed off the ladder. I've made some great music and moved people, and that's what it's all about. You don't play notes in music—you play emotion." ●

LR017

KENNY YOUNG

At the end of the day
What can you say?

— KING OF KINGS, "WRITTEN ALL OVER YOU"

KENNY YOUNG never had it easy. He was born in 1966 and abandoned by his parents. He went unadopted until age five, and then grew up with his new family in the normalcy of suburban Long Island. He was handsome and fashionable, and demonstrated graphic arts and graffiti abilities at Valley Stream High School, where he inspired many, including future TV celebrity Fred Armisen. Kenny brought Fred to New York City to buy punk vinyl and to see shows, and the two played in a spiky-haired band, The KGB, that opened for G.B.H. and Murphy's Law at Rock Hotel in 1984. Young moved to the city later that year to attend Fashion Institute of Technology. There he dove into the most intense New York hardcore music, befriending his hero Dave Insurgent of Reagan Youth.

Young quickly tired of punk conformity and expressed his love for prog-rock bands like Gong and Magma when he formed the avant-garde, neo-psychedelic group, King of Kings. With extended jams, elaborate costumes, a 6'5"

crooning golem named Dank, and sets at times featuring up to three Gong covers, King of Kings were the unlikeliest NYC rock band of 1986–87.

Young became a top-notch bassist comprable to Chris Squire or John Wetton. He renamed himself "Desmond Horn" and stripped down King of Kings to a power trio, with Greco-American drum whiz Gus Hart and guitarist Kevin Gerber.

Frank Hannon of Tesla saw them play The Limelight in 1990. He phoned his Geffen A&R man Tom Zutaut (Guns N'Roses, Mötley Crüe), who flew in the next day to check out the band. Upon hearing gems such as "Seasons of Eve" and "Auto-Magick," Zutaut deemed Kenny Young a musical genius, and signed King of Kings on the spot.

John Cobbett replaced guitarist Kevin Gerber, and then Kevin "Shantytown" O'Neill replaced Cobbett. The band moved to Los Angeles to work with Queen producer Roy Thomas Baker. Geffen was talking big. Unfortunately, Young's excesses and addictions

Kenny Young with Tibbie X, New York, 2011. Selfie by Kenny Young.
Courtesy of the friends of Kenny Young.

record is the ultimate show of disrespect by a label and the ultimate humiliation for an artist. That contributed to Young's downward spiral. *Guru's* guitarist Christian Kegler overdosed and died a few months after the album got nixed.

Young got deeper into drugs but he couldn't always handle them. Following a string of busts, the LAPD forced him to work as a snitch. He couldn't handle that either. He got out from under the cops' control and made it back to NYC, where he spent the next decade doing solo gigs, working occasionally as a Wilhelmina model, and then running an early hipster clothing line, Grandville. In 2005, he managed to land a publishing deal with MCA. MCA expected something heavy; Young's sound had softened over the years, and disappointed the publisher. The deal fell apart.

Kenny Young was a true punk who got expelled from the rock kingdom. He defied conventional wisdom by not trying to be the next Kurt Cobain. And he didn't want to be the tattooed, millionaire, record-industry shill playing corporate Super Bowl parties—he couldn't be that person. Young suffered the fate of many tormented artists. He repeatedly pressed the self-destruct button.

quickly became apparent. That doomed him and his band. His erratic antics and intoxication rituals quickly became staples of LA rock lore.

So, in 1991, a few months after the epoch-defining new sounds of Nirvana were first heard, came *King of Kings*, an over-the-top prog opus that fell on deaf ears in the newly-minted grunge era. It was an incredible piece of work, like a modern-day Yes or Emerson Lake & Palmer album. It received some nice press, but all the big dogs, like MTV and *Rolling Stone*, refused to bite.

Geffen funded King of Kings for 1993's *Who's Your Guru?* It was a stirring effort, recorded with Carole King producer Chris Rankin and Guns N' Roses engineer Jim Mitchell. The sound was melodic and moody, just like Kenny Young. But the label deemed the 12 songs unsellable, shelved the record, and dropped the band. Shelving a

Young spent the next few years married, divorced, working as a pimp, dealing drugs, and doing graphic art. For a while, he lived with other junkies in the notorious 9th floor drug den at 4 West 22nd Street (subject of Jessica Dimmock's documentary *The 9th Floor*). His luck eventually ran out. He'd been given many opportunities but frittered them away—major label contracts, high-priced modeling deals, acting offers, artistic opportunities, rich girlfriends—and there he was rotting away in a junkie hellhole.

Despite his problems, he attempted to get back in the game. In 2010, in a strange twist of fate, Young replaced his hero Dave Insurgent as the vocalist

Kenny Young, "Bow Wow, Kenny with his Pomeranian," New York, 2003. Polaroid Color 668 by Gail Thacker. Courtesy of Gail Thacker.

of Reagan Youth (Dave had committed suicide several years earlier, after the murder of his prostitute girlfriend by serial killer Joel Rifkin). That was a great opportunity, given the renewed interest in 80s-style hardcore music. Needless to say, he wrecked it all by smoking crack constantly while on tour. His drug addiction, his bouts with infectious diseases, and his near-death encounters once again led him to the gutter.

Kenny Young was a troubled soul. He'd lived his nine lives. Old age was never in the cards. By 2012,

his veins turned to scar tissue and his asthmatic lungs were destroyed by crack—he had reached the end of the line. His ravaged body was found April 2, 2014.

Before he died, Young wrote to his friend Glenn Max, "I look the same. My art chops are tight. But my spirit is so fucking wounded, desouled by this life. I've had to be such a bastard at times. It's hard to believe I was even capable of some of that. I seemed to have left all that behind for some time now. That's good." ●

MARGE RAYMOND

There's a million worlds and so many
lives to choose
So I turn around like a fool and came
to take you

— FLAME, "MIDNIGHT SUN"

MARGE RAYMOND had everything it took to be a rock star. She got discovered at age 14 singing doo-wop on Avenue D in East Flatbush, Brooklyn, and signed to Coed Records. 1965's girl-group-style "Sad Illusion" b/w "You Better Get what Goes for You," as Margie & The Formations, peaked on the *Billboard* charts at #22. From that one-hit-wonder status, the childhood friend of Evie Sands became an in-demand Brill Building session singer for the next several years.

In 1971 she formed a trio called SuMagNa—a blending of the names Susan Collins, Marge Raymond, and Nancy O'Neil—that signed to Don Kirshner Entertainment with a young Paul Shaffer assigned as their musical director. SuMagNa became top session and touring vocalists, traveling harmoniously with New Riders of the Purple Sage and Electric Light Orchestra. Raymond sang on ELO's *Face the Music* and their 1975 smash "Evil Woman." The future looked bright.

Jimmy Iovine engineered ELO's sessions. One night, he and Raymond shared a cab ride, during which he told the sexy singer that she

should front her own rock band. So Iovine helped her form Flame. He got her a songwriting deal with Warner/Chappel and the band signed to RCA. Guests on 1976's *Flame* and 1977's *Queen of the Neighborhood* LPs included Clarence Clemens, Steve Van Zandt, and Luther Vandross. Flame toured with heavy-duty arena-rockers of the day like Foreigner and Bachman-Turner Overdrive. But RCA dropped the ball, so Flame burned out while recording a third album.

Undeterred, she and her Flame-guitarist boyfriend Jimmy Crespo—armed with a blazing eight-song demo—signed with Aerosmith managers Steve Leber and David Krebs. At that time Aerosmith was at its nadir. They needed a new guitarist to replace Joe Perry, and Crespo fit the bill. Through those circles, Marge met the members of a hard rock trio; they joined forces as Kicks, and became Aersomith's opening act. Steven Tyler had Raymond join him onstage, doing background vocals.

Aerosmith's internal problems—Tyler's drug use, for example—led to drummer Joey Kramer forming a new band, Renegade, with Raymond as singer, guitarist Jimmy Crespo, bassist Tom Hamilton, and Peter Frampton keyboardist Bob Mayo. Renegade laid down basic tracks for seven songs at NYC's SIR Studios, and showcased it for CBS. Tyler caught wind of what was going on and got it together enough to reinvigorate Aerosmith, so Renegade got shelved.

Raymond then tried going solo, backed by Kicks members, plus Steve Augeri, later the singer for Journey. That went nowhere. In the 80s metal era, she fronted Proton. They did an album at The Hit Factory, and then broke up after their drummer died. She also sang on, and composed for, albums by Humble Pie, Elephant's Memory, Billion Dollar Babies, and Helen Schneider. Those gigs were good but they left her unsatisfied and unfulfilled. It was time to rethink her musical outlook.

The singer then pursued her love of classical music. She joined Collegiate Chorale, backup chorus for Luciano Pavarotti's *Pavarotti Plus* concerts on PBS and at the Richard Tucker Gala with Metropolitan Opera stars. She intrigued Pavarotti as his female first tenor.

In 1990, she joined Generation Gap, an eight-piece with horns and a 1,300-song repertoire, playing corporate events, dinner clubs, weddings, and Bar Mitzvahs. She sang cabaret at The Duplex. She did Off-Broadway theater with the Gotham Rock Choir, and at many benefits, like for Hurricane Sandy relief and shows with Rockers in Recovery. For the past 25 years she's given weekly tours of Brooklyn's historic Green-Wood Cemetery.

Marge Raymond said of her hard-rocking ways: "There was no marketing formula for a female front person in a rock band. Everyone was at a loss as to how to successfully promote me. I was one of the first to do what I did!" ●

Top: *Flame*, RCA, 1976. Marge Raymond sang for the first major label female-fronted hard rock band. Bottom: Marge Raymond recording for the musical *Xstar* by Peppy Castro (Blues Magoos), 2008. Images courtesy of Marge Raymond.

LR019

JAKE HOLMES

I'm dazed and confused, is it stay, is it go? I'm being abused, and I think I should know

— JAKE HOLMES, "DAZED AND CONFUSED"

JAKES HOLMES wrote and recorded one of the most famous songs in rock history, but was never given credit—you know the song, and you know the famous band that stole it.

Jake was too stiff for the hippie era—not funky enough for the time's tie-dyed zeitgeist—and when he did catch up, his hippie-ish persona didn't fit the hard-rocking 70s. Holmes had all the elements for success—big-time management, major labels, mainstream media coverage—but somehow the dots never connected. As his career progressed, he worked with the biggest stars in the industry, but the acclaim always went to someone else.

John Greer Holmes, Jr. was born December 8, 1939 in San Francisco and raised on Long Island. After graduating high school, he joined The Lyric Theater in Piermont, New York, an experimental opera company where in 1962 he and his first wife Kay Allen met and put together a folk parody act, Allen & Grier, which played the Village folk clubs and shared management with The Serendipity Singers.

"My career started at The Lyric Theater. We'd do all sorts of weird stuff. Our composer, Henry Brant, was a Charles Ives disciple, and he'd do stuff like have one band playing one song march toward another band on the other side of the room playing another song, and the audience would be in the middle, and the musicians would try to cross through. At The Lyric Theater I met this girl who ended up being my wife. We became Allen & Grier. She was a classical pianist/singer going to Bennington, so I was hanging out up there, playing piano for dance classes. I'd sleep in the girls' dormitory and then sneak out in the morning. That's how we started our act."

The duo, in which Kay sang sardonically and Jake strummed guitar, recorded 1963's caustic album *It's Better to be Rich than Ethnic* (FM/Vee Jay) and did two songs for *The World of Folk*

Jake Holmes' first album. Allen & Grier, *Better to Be Rich than Ethnic*, FM/Vee-Jay, live at The Bitter End, 1963. Collection of the author.

Music compilation with folk diehards like Fred Neil, Len Chandler, Bob Carey, and The Big Three (Mama Cass Elliot, Tim Rose, and James Hendricks). Pete Seeger assailed Allen & Grier in *Sing Out!* magazine as the most tasteless group he'd ever seen. The group generated a buzz on the scene until Jake got drafted.

"We formed that act and went down to a hootenanny at The Bitter End. I knew about three chords on the guitar and we had a couple of funny songs. Fred Weintraub, The Bitter End's owner, liked us and said if we could come up with five songs, he'd put us on as an opening act. In those days at The Bitter End they had three acts: the main act would be the draw, the second main act which was a sort-of draw, and then the opening act would be a nobody who they'd hope would develop a draw over time. It was a very good system. There was this strong nexus of music and comedy and politics there at the time. We ended

up being managed by Fred and making our album *It's Better to Be Rich than Ethnic* with these parody folk songs. We really were tasteless! But that's what we were about, poking fun at folk music.

"Then I get drafted into the Army and my partner Kay left me for our other manager Roy Silver, who managed Bill Cosby, and they went off to California. I was devastated. When I got out of the Army, I started playing in some rock bands. I was up in Canada working with this group, and a French girl I was dating at the time convinced me to start doing my own songs. So I started playing The Bitter End again and writing serious songs."

Jake's folk scene cache won him work with folk-rock star Tim Rose's band.

"I worked with Tim Rose. First we were called The Thorns. Then it became Tim Rose & The Thorns. We decided we were going to do folk-rock so we took folk songs and did them in a rock and roll style. Tim's signature song was 'Hey Joe' which was the version Jimi Hendrix heard, and we did a heavy version of The Kingston Trio's 'Tom Dooley.' We played quite often in the Village at The Night Owl."

The Bitter End's Fred Weintraub (later producer of films such as *Woodstock* and *Enter the Dragon*) asked Jake to join a cabaret/comedy act he was starting and managing. The trio, called Jim, Jake, and Joan, consisted of comics Jim Connell and Joan Rivers, with Jake as the straight man. Jim, Jake, and Joan appeared in the 1965 film *Once Upon a Coffee House*. They all ended up enemies.

"Fred Weintraub was friends with Albert Grossman, who put together Peter, Paul & Mary as a pop group. That's where Fred got the idea for The Serendipity Singers and The Bitter End Singers. He decided to put me, Joan Rivers, and Jim Connell together as a trio, but Joan was a pain in the ass. Once, we did this benefit for Bobby Kennedy. She and Jim did not get along, and they got into it. They were always arguing and jostling for space, and I was literally in the middle. After that benefit, she never spoke to either of us again. We'd go onstage and she'd be cheerful and interact, and then as soon as we got off stage, nothing. Then, if we were doing interviews she was our best friend, and then afterwards nothing, so we didn't last long. What made her good was she was truly mean and nasty. In her biography she called me 'a wound with a tie,' which I didn't understand. I knew I was a bit down and angst-ridden but I don't think I ever wore a tie."

As the early 60s turned into the late 60s, social norms changed. Jake was a tall and strapping presence, a little too "normal" for those shaggy times. "My first marijuana experience," Jake relates, "I was totally freaked out. I thought I was gonna die. That's how weird it was. I was a wimp. I was a nerd. I couldn't commit myself to getting stoned-out and freaked-out and joining a cult and singing on the streets. I liked hot, running water and TV—and I still do."

Jake's debut solo album, 1967's *The Above Ground Sound of Jake Holmes* (Tower)—the title a riff on the emerging underground scene, with Jake wearing a suit on the cover—spawned two minor singles: "You Can't Get Love" b/w "Think I'm Being Had" and "Genuine Imitation Life" b/w "Hard to Keep My Mind on You." The album was sold as a stereo recording but the stereo mix got misplaced, so buyers got a mono mix transferred to duophonic.

"I never felt part of that 'in' thing. That's what *The Above Ground Sound* was about. I was apart from it as opposed to a part of it. That wasn't really true—I was there and I was in it. But there were a lot of guys like me, like Van Dyke Parks and Tim Buckley, on the edges. It's not that we were less

Jim, Jake & Joan (Jake Holmes with comedians Jim Connell and Joan Rivers). Photo by James J. Kriegsmann, 1964. Courtesy of Jake Holmes.

talented. It's that we weren't plugged into the vibration. We were outside the vibration. I feel I was lucky I didn't get into that. It may have killed some people, like Buckley.

"I was saying that I wasn't taking all this too seriously. I loved to do comedy, I loved theater and I loved jazz, and I loved all this stuff that was counter-intuitive to this folk-rock, down-in-the-dirt thing. I kind of felt like, 'I'm a WASP from Long Island, why am I trying to be some funky guy?' I just felt like I couldn't do that honestly. I wasn't trying to be so heavy—it wasn't in my DNA. I was off the trail. I just had to do my own thing and hope people would dig it. I was basically a lyric-driven writer. I think I got over with my lyrics. That's what I was gunning for."

Jake Holmes, "Dazed and Confused"
promotional single, Tower Records, 1967.
The song that Led Zeppelin stole.
Courtesy of Jake Holmes

To push the album, Jake played a three-week stint at The Bitter End, and promoted it with a set on *The Tonight Show* with guest host Woody Allen. Jake joked to Woody, his good friend and fellow Bitter End habitué, "Yeah, I'm packing them in with my big name."

"I'm grateful now because in the success that I've had—I was on *The Tonight Show* and did lots of stuff—I was miserable. That was the most miserable time of my life. It was horrible. One part of me wishes I'd succeeded in that way, but the other part of me is grateful because I got to live life in a more substantive way. I wasn't separated from it. I worked with some big celebrities, and what I learned is none of them are happy. They're miserable and I know that feeling; you're constantly

trying to hold on to what you've got. When you don't have it, you don't have to hold on anymore.

"It's the dichotomy of the American dream: wanting all this material success, and at the same time trying to keep your integrity. You're constantly being pulled. I didn't have the strength of character necessary to play the game. At that time it would've messed me up badly. The same thing with cocaine—for some reason in all those crazy years, no one ever offered me any. I mean, I smoked a lot of grass, but it made me nuts and paranoid, and I had to stop. In the 80s my heart stopped—I had the same thing as that NBA player Len Bias—and had I been doing cocaine I would've died. So just who is it out there looking out for me? The cocaine I never got exposed to was some sort of sign."

I'm dazed and confused, there's something all wrong They're tellin' me Jimmy Page wrote this song

— JAKE HOLMES, "DAZED AND CONFUSED 2010"

ON AUGUST 25, 1967, Jake played at The Village Theater (which later became The Fillmore East) on a bill with The Yardbirds and Jesse Colin Young. Yardbirds guitarist Jimmy Page saw Jake move the crowd with his song "Dazed and Confused" and sent someone to Bleecker Bob's record shop to buy *The Above Ground Sound*. 1968's *Live Yardbirds* included a version of the song with Jake's lyrics and arrangement, listed as "I'm Confused" with no ascribed credits. The only visual documentation of them doing it was March 9, 1968 on French TV's *Baton Rouge*. Page updated "Dazed and Confused" on 1969's *Led Zeppelin*.

"I wrote 'Dazed and Confused' with the trio on *The Above Ground Sound*. It became our signature song. The song had that 6/8 descending thing. I didn't know it was a fresh and original idea; I just did it. We played it at that show and blew the place apart. That's when Jimmy Page saw it, and from what I gather from guys in The Yardbirds now, Page sent someone out to get my album and they began to do it. The Yardbirds did my version of it. When Page went to Led Zeppelin, he tweaked the lyrics and did a great job—he picked it up a notch, I can't argue that—but he certainly ripped me off.

"I wrote Page a letter once and said, 'You don't need to do this. Nobody's going to think less of you if you give half the credit to someone. In fact, they may think more of you. It gives you more credibility to say, 'Here's what I can do with your song.' You're perfectly talented; you don't need to take credit. God knows you're brilliant—stop!'"

Holmes has mixed feelings regarding Led Zeppelin. "I don't hate them. I had experience with a lot of those English rock bands. I had arrogance about what I was doing. I never thought of myself as a rock and roller, I was more artsy than that. So I was kind of out of it. Sometimes I think of all that money I could've gotten from suing those guys earlier. But I did okay in life; it's not like I'm a poor bum wino. If I were, I'd be pretty pissed off. The blues guys like Willie Dixon really deserved the money.

"I took what I'd call positive revenge, writing a new 'Dazed and Confused.' It's now: 'I'm dazed and confused, there's something all wrong/They're telling me Jimmy Page wrote this song/1968 that's where it's at/Well I wrote this damn thing a year before that.' I even thought about doing it with their arrangement and saying, 'Here, sue me!' I get credibility and mileage from having written the song. Street cred is a form of payment. I have enough to live the way I live. I have a nice house I bought at a good price and a great wife and kids, I'm don't need to live a $400,000-a-year life. I write music because it's what I love."

Holmes' tortuous 1968 follow-up, *A Letter to Katherine December* (Tower), addressed his painful divorce from first wife Kay. The overlooked Elliot Mazer-produced LP included the dour opus "Saturday Night," which went into light rotation in a few markets.

"The next album was based on my wife leaving me. That's when I met Elliot Mazer, a very cool producer, and we worked with a great arranger, Charlie Fox. We went to RCA Studios and recorded everything on film. That was interesting because film was cleaner than tape. It was almost like recording digital. That stuff was really out there, it was like Van Dyke Parks or something. But I wasn't thinking 'experimental,' it was just a free-working environment. I love that album—it was so nutty and off-the-wall."

1969's Mazer-produced *Jake Holmes* (Polydor) got recorded in Nashville and sounded like it, with twang galore. A *Village Voice* ad (2/5/70) offered consumers the chance to receive a promo single of "How Are You (Part One)" b/w "How Are You (Part Two)" by sending "Ten cents, 10¢, one dime or two nickels for this 45 RPM" to Polydor's 1700 Broadway office. The previous year, *Voice* scribe Robert Christgau lumped Jake in with other Dylan-istas: "The vocal limitations, I would guess, are related to what is really a disdain for music. As for the songs—well, never mind." Then came 1970's *So Close, So Very Far to Go* (Polydor) with his biggest chart hit, a sensitive lilt, "So Close," that cracked the Top 40 for a few weeks that summer:

"We did *Jake Holmes* at Cinderella Studios in Nashville with [Neil Young producer] David Briggs and Wayne Moss, and those guys were

great. I loved that album. Then David and Norbert Putnam opened up Quadraphonic Studios and we did *So Close*. The song 'So Close' was very interesting because it was one of those songs that took a few weeks for people to warm up to. Then a few key stations dropped it right before it made real impact. At that point there were all these wonderful ballads on the chart. I think that's what killed that record."

Expecting a future star, Clive Davis lured Jake to Columbia Records. 1971's *How Much Time*, produced by Susan Hamilton, yielded "Trust Me" b/w "Just as Lost as Me" and "Silence" b/w "How Much Time"—but no hits. He pushed the album touring with Pacific Gas & Electric and James Cotton Blues Band. Before Columbia axed him, Jake recorded at Quadraphonic again, this time with his Nashville friend David Briggs.

"Most of the lyrics back then were that 'elusive butterfly of love' kind of crap. I did this song in Nashville with the lyrics 'boredom creeps in on vanilla feet.' David Briggs never let me forget that one. But I do realize that every once in a while I did get pretty out-of-hand with the poetry. That 'let's get artsy' spirit was in the air."

For that laidback recording, Jake played European dates with rowdy, bluesy hard rock bands. "I did a tour of England," Jake recalls, "and started getting recognition. I toured with Rory Gallagher and Stone the Crows and got blown off the stage. I was touring without a drummer doing this folk-ish sound and these unruly crowds came there looking for something heavy duty. So the reaction was sometimes very bad. But in the end it was a great and successful time."

So close, I almost couldn't see you
So close, but it looks like we're alright

— JAKE HOLMES, "SO CLOSE"

IN ADDITION TO BEING a singer-songwriter, Jake got into producing records. His first job was The Four Seasons' 1969, *Sgt. Pepper's*-style album *Genuine Imitation Life Gazette*. The album's title was inspired by Jake's song "Genuine Imitation Life," which Four Season Bob Gaudio saw Holmes perform at The Bitter End.

"Yes, The Four Seasons wanted to do their *Sgt. Pepper's*," Jake recalls. "They wanted Four Seasons-gone-art. We had the same manager, so they called 'the artsy guy.' I'd hang out with the comedians in front of The Bitter End and one night a limo pulls up. One of them joked, 'Is that yours?' So I jumped in and drove away—it was Bob Gaudio picking me up to write with him in Jersey. That was the one time I out-comedianed the comedians.

"We really worked together well. It was a great collaboration. But that album was a tad too baroque. It was like Phil Spector when he worked with Leonard Cohen. Bobby is a wonderfully talented man, but he's no Phil Spector and I'm not Leonard Cohen. But it was the same type of marriage of two disparate artistic forces. We came up with some great music, like the song 'Genuine Imitation Life Gazette,' which had a lot of that baroque lyric writing. But The Four Seasons were The Four Seasons; they didn't need to do that. The album included a 'Genuine Imitation Life Gazette' insert with pictures and words. It should be a collector's item. The package was incredible."

Next, Holmes and Gaudio wrote and produced *Watertown*, Frank Sinatra's final (and lowest-selling) record. A UPI wire story best described the unconventional quasi-concept album: "On the surface *Watertown* seems a slow, almost monotonous work. Yet there are suggestions of wilder beats, and the seeds of a psychedelic sound."

"Writing with Bob was tough because he made me write to his melodies. And I was not used to that. I was used to going back and forth and amending melodies here and there. So it was a

Jake Homes, *So Close, So Very Far to Go*, Polydor, 1970. Photography and design by Bob Cato. Collection of the author.

Left: Jake Holmes, leading a songwriting workshop, New York, 2011. Courtesy of Jake Holmes

Right: Jake Holmes and Harry Belafonte, during the making of Harry's *Paradise in Gazankulu*, EMI, 1988. Uncredited snapshot. Courtesy of Jake Holmes.

tough gig. Anyway, Bobby became friends with Sinatra. When he got the gig, I suggested we do a concept album that tells a story all the way through. They loved that idea. So we ended up with *Watertown*. That was not baroque; it was very jazz-theater style. It's the story of a man whose woman is away and then she leaves him. When I toured England, the press asked me if this story was about Sinatra and Mia Farrow and I'd feign ignorance. It wasn't, but it was fine for them to think it was.

"Sinatra was wonderful; he was so great to us. He was very respectful to lyricists. He'd come to me with a lead sheet and ask if he could change a word here or there. I was so impressed with him because when he'd sing a song, he really paid attention to the words he was singing. He wasn't one of those guys smiling when he was singing; he listened to the story of the lyrics. He was the only performer I know that credited songwriters and arrangers onstage. So he was a songwriter's best friend, for lots of reasons. Our problem was, his voice was shot. He was not singing up to his level."

When asked on a 1975 TV episode of *The Cousin Brucie Show* about his songwriting work for Sinatra, Jake answered, "I would say 90 percent of my songs are either portraits of people that I know or part of myself projected into someone else."

High school hero is no more
He's working at the grocery store

— JAKE HOLMES, "HIGH SCHOOL HERO"

HOLMES COULD NEVER CONNECT with a hit single, but his clever lyrics and ability to turn a phrase made him ideal for Madison Avenue. There he found success as a jingle writer, first with the jingle house HEA Productions and then as partner in his own firms, Three Tree Music and Four/Four Productions. He was behind advertising classics, such as "Be All You Can Be," "Be a Pepper," "Gillette: the Best a Man Can Get," "Aren't You Hungry for Burger King Now?" and "Raise Your Hands if You're Sure."

Jake speaks of applying his problem-solving abilities to jingle writing: "Where I had my most success, in terms of financial success, was writing jingles and doing commercials. And that was the biggest lie of all. But I was able to step out of that problem; I was able to do something that didn't deal with all that truth. When I sang my first commercial, I had a completely different vocal ease because it was a song that I wrote for them. So I didn't have the pressure in my voice. Once I started doing commercials, I loosened up.

"My first commercial was an anti-drug commercial. 'What do you do when the music stops? Where are you then?' I loved doing it; it was a challenge, like doing puzzles. Plus I love to play in all sorts of genres, which I can't really do as a solo artist. It was a way to learn a craft by writing short tunes that had to fit a logo or product. It was quite scientific. To this day I enjoy doing it. It was much more civilized work than going on the road and struggling with promoters and

record labels who rip you off. If I believed in him, I would thank God that I got into that field.

"During the time Vietnam was going, I refused to do commercials for the Army. Then after Vietnam they came up with this great line, 'Army: Be All You Can Be.' My feeling was if we're building a volunteer Army, we should keep the volunteers at the highest levels. I didn't feel like I was going against anything. As a matter of fact, in retrospect, there's a quality to it and a respect for the Army. The fact is, that anti-Army 60s and 70s thing has changed. People understand we need a protective force that's a force for good. I feel that's been proven out. Of course there's been bad actions, too. I've gone through phases of wondering whether what I did was right. When I was on *Oprah* she said, 'There must be lots of guys in the Army mad at you for that commercial...' But by and large I feel it was a force for good, not a force for bad.

"One of my jingle-writing partners used to say that we were one of the last vestiges of commissioned art. As time's gone on, the lines have blurred between commercial music and pop music. Everybody's trying for the same thing, to make money by writing tunes. Back when I started writing jingles, the lines were not blurred. When I started out, I didn't want to sing on commercials because I felt it would hurt my singing career. I recall the Chevy singers made $15,000 one year and I made $2,000 for writing it. So I stopped worrying about that very fast. There is no difference. I always took writing jingles as seriously as I did any song. I desperately tried to

Jake Holmes, still making music, Towne Crier, Beacon, New York, March 2015. Photo by William Lulow. Courtesy of Jake Holmes.

make them as good as possible. All the ad slogans we wrote around were almost song lines in themselves. So it's about making it more than just a line in a commercial; it's almost a song. There are some ads I'm really proud of, like Gillette. I think 'The Best a Man Can Get' is a really strong piece of music. The other thing is, I've gotten to work with many great musicians in advertising."

Jake's friend Harry Belafonte counters: "I think the greatest example of a success that has haunted Jake is 'Be All You Can Be,' that commercial he wrote for the Army. You'll never meet anyone more anti-violent than Jake—the most resistant to the idea of war—yet here he wrote this fiercely successful commercial for recruiting young men to join the military to go kill themselves or kill others. I think having done that annoyed Jake. It expressed the power of his gift to write in a style to make that appealing—it made him understand the kind of responsibility that came with that gift. Then he's written all these other songs that make you want to go out and buy one and kill yourself

after you consume it for a few years. There are all these contradictions, but our society is filled with such contradictions. We all fall prey to it one way or another. It's a contamination I'm unsure you can avoid."

The Belafonte connection began after Harry recorded a few of Jake's songs. The most successful of those was Harry's 1986 minor hit duet with Jennifer Warnes, "Skin to Skin." That musical reliability led to Harry hiring Jake as his musical director. The two also worked on original music for a Belafonte TV show that never materialized.

"Trust is something you build and faith is something you acquire," Belafonte muses. "I saw in him a touch of incredible genius. So I took great faith in his talent. I took faith in his gift. I took faith in his sensibilities. I could walk in as a person of color, coming from these very specific experiences—and some of mine have been particularly intense because I've always been an activist, so I'm always looking to move into the eye of the hurricane—and for this young, WASP-ish, thin, strange, white kid to be walking into the same blizzard or typhoon; it's been great to see Jake evolve. He also has his own sense of justice and essential fairness and he became personally engaged with what I was trying to do. He found that his voice was a multiple instrument, effectively writing in patterns unlike his cultural history. He had an incredible capacity to adapt, which is quite stunning. To this day he takes on many different styles because he needs to have these experiences."

Belafonte, banned in 80s apartheid South Africa for his activism, sent Jake and arranger Richard Cummings as tourists to write and record with musicians like Makgona Tsohle, Brenda Fassie, and The Soul Brothers. Jake and Richard got trailed and grilled by police, so after each session, they'd smuggle the tapes to EMI's local office, who sent them on to London. Holmes produced, co-wrote, and played a mix of electronic, African, and European instruments on *Paradise in Gazankulu*, Harry's 1988 world music album that *Voice* critic Robert Christgau hailed as "a very hot piece of assimilationist mbaqanga."

"I wasn't as political as I am now," Jake reflects. "It wasn't until I started working with Harry Belafonte and went to South Africa and really got involved with him that I became much more politicized and much more aware. I didn't get emotionally involved in the civil rights movement until after it was happening, until it was safe."

Belafonte: "The fact that Jake would brave all that, and face that potential anguish—he could have gone to jail and gotten lost in the legal maze in the center of the belly of the beast of racial rage of white South Africans, who were every bit as cruel as the Nazi machine. So, Jake going there to write songs that critiqued those people who did all that evil, and praising young men and women of color for defying the system—he did all that— he really put himself in harm's way. But in the final analysis, I think he did it because he felt he had to. He felt it was a calling for his gift."

In 2010, *TMZ* reported that a lawsuit Jake brought against Jimmy Page and Led Zeppelin was settled out of court, meaning no one can publicly comment on the specifics. At the time of this writing, Jake is composing a musical about the 60s generation. He writes indie film soundtracks and jams at the Lower East Side poetry venue The Nuyorican Cafe.

"There are some people, unlike me, who have the smarts to know how to cut into it," Jake reflects. "They discover their artistic formula or find ways to schmooze. It's definitely a skill to cut into the fame thing. I don't have the personality for it. I'm shy in the wrong sort of way. It takes a type of emotional unconsciousness, and I'm inhibited in ways that stop me. I have a self-destructive thing against fame; every time it appears, I try to get away from it. I fear it."

"He's never lost his naivety," Belafonte adds. "There's an innocence that gives Jake a capacity to write the way he does. Much of what he writes is poetically vulnerable; he has a spirit behind the language that he evokes that's astounding. It's that contradiction that makes him such a great writer. He writes to conflict so well. I listen to the pros and cons in his prose, and he writes a thought against a thought. He'd be a great playwright."

Jake: "I remember when I opened for The Carpenters. It was great but it was too big. I like a party where there are six people at a table and they're all drinking and having a good time and talking and everybody's communicating. That's what my kind of performing is about: communicating and feeling that pushback, where people are really conscious of what you're doing. It's all about connecting with words and sound."

Belafonte: "Some artists feel that being commercially successful requires feeding a grist mill irrelevant things. Jake doesn't like to feed the grist-mill of success and go through that shit. He'd rather be up in the countryside than in the hub of all this activity that grinds you under. Some guys become stars because they catch a lucky moment in life, when their gift is fully expressed, and it explodes, and you have no choice but to gravitate towards that dynamic force. Jake doesn't have that combustion. He's coming from another place that's far more reserved. He has to reveal himself to you. You don't see him."

Jake: "I remember Harry said to me one day, 'I'm authentic.' He had just realized it. All of his life he never felt authentic. And I think that's something I really fought with too." ●

SOURCES

All interviews by Steven Blush — either solo for this book
or with Paul Rachman and Tony Mann for a documentary
film production — unless otherwise noted.

BOBBY JAMESON: San Luis Obispo, CA, 2009, 2011
GLORIA JONES: New York, NY, 2008
DAVID PEEL: New York, NY, 2009, 2010
CHRIS ROBISON: Danbury, Connecticut, 2009, New York, NY, 2011
GASS WILD and **JOHNNY HODGE**: New York, NY, 2010, 2012
CHERRY VANILLA: Hollywood, CA, 2011
EVIE SANDS: Studio City, CA 2009, 2010
JAKE HOLMES: New York, NY 2010, 2011
BILL LASWELL: New York, NY, 2008
MICHAEL ALAGO: New York, NY, 2010
ROLAN BOLAN: Los Angeles, CA, 2010
BRIAN KEHEW: Los Angeles, CA, 2010
CHIP TAYLOR: New York, NY, 2011
AL GARGONI: New York, NY, 2011
HARRY BELAFONTE: New York, NY, 2010
LEMMY KILMISTER: Sayreville, NJ, 2011
GINGER BIANCO: New York, NY, 2010
PAT BRIGGS: via email, 2015
CHRIS DARROW: via email, 2015
BETTY DAVIS: *Dazed* (UK), by Jessica Hundley, 2007
CHARLIE FARREN: *Oocities*, by Mark Blair, 1999
ROBERT FLEISHMAN: phone interview, 2015
RIK FOX: *Record Connection*, 1997
ALAN MERRILL: New York, NY, 2015
MARGE RAYMOND: New York, NY, 2013
RICK RIVETS: via email, 2015
BRETT SMILEY: *(H)ear*, by Carson Arnold, 2003
KENNY YOUNG: Letter to Glenn Max, 2008